Paying the Price

The Untold Story
of the Iranian Resistance

L Todd Wood

Paying the Price

The Untold Story
of the Iranian Resistance

VINDICTA

Vindicta Publishing

Las Vegas ♦ Chicago ♦ Palm Beach

Published in the United States of America by
Histria Books
7181 N. Hualapai Way, Ste. 130-86
Las Vegas, NV 89166 U.S.A.
HistriaBooks.com

Vindicta Publishing is an imprint of Histria Books and a joint venture of Histria Books and Creative Destruction Media. Titles published under the imprints of Histria Books are distributed worldwide.

Library of Congress Control Number: 2023938051

ISBN 978-1-59211-350-7 (hardcover)
ISBN 978-1-59211-361-3 (eBook)

Preface

I decided to write this book six years ago after being introduced to members of the People's Mujahadeen of Iran, or Mujahadeen-e-Khalq in Paris, France. I was introduced through a friend who was involved in the Free Iran rally in the summer of that year.

I consider myself a traveled and educated person. I've done business in over forty countries, traveled to many more while in the military, including time in the Middle East, and during a long stint on Wall Street.

However, when confronted with the existence of the PMOI/MEK, I had to admit to myself I had never heard of them.

Why is that? I asked myself.

As I investigated this question, I found out there was a very good reason for this situation — a concerted and extremely successful disinformation campaign by the Iranian Ministry of Intelligence and successive administrations of the United States government.

This piqued my curiosity to dig even more. Who were these people? Why were they so persecuted? Why did the Iranian government want them killed? In other words, *why was the Iranian government so scared of them?*

In contrast to the incompetence and arrogance of the George W. Bush administration, and the outright treachery of the Obama administration, the Mujahadeen can actually say they have been right about the Middle East all along. The MEK warned Bush that Iran would use the Iraq War to cement control over the entire region if the U.S. wasn't careful in Iraq. The warnings were ignored.

The Obama administration tried as hard as it could to allow the MEK to be killed — before the courts, Congress, and public opinion forced their relocation to Albania in 2016.

Even today, the Iranian MOIS (Ministry of Intelligence) is repeatedly trying to destroy the MEK on foreign soil.

I spent weeks with the MEK in their headquarters in Paris, and in their Camp Ashraf 3 in Albania. I was the first Western journalist to visit the camp.

We will go into depth on all of these points. However, I guarantee one thing: you will learn a lot from the book, much you did not know — or should I say, weren't *permitted* to know.

As thousands of Iranian teenagers are being murdered as we speak in Iranian cities by the mullahs, I hope this book resonates with the free world.

L Todd Wood

Introduction

Born from revolution under the Shah, the MEK believed they were going to share power with the mullahs in Iran after the fall of the monarch — to build a new Persian society, free of tyranny.

They were wrong.

The mullahs, bent on total control, savagely oppressed the MEK and do still to this day. Over 130,000 members have been executed by the regime, a large percentage children and a large percentage female.

To counter this oppression, the MEK built a powerful military force on the Iraqi border. They miraculously acquired three hundred armored vehicles and trained ten thousand soldiers, many of whom were female.

Incursions from this Iraqi base, including Operation Eternal Light, severely threatened the mullahs' grip on power.

Unfortunately, the U.S. military during the first Gulf War, disarmed the MEK, labeled them terrorists, abandoned their protection under the Geneva Convention, and allowed Iraqi forces to murder at will with infantry assaults and missile attacks.

The U.S. Department of State acted nefariously during these murders, abandoning the U.S. responsibility it acquired when it guaranteed the MEK protection under the Geneva Convention.

Eventually, public pressure forced Washington to relocate the remaining three thousand combatants to Albania, where the majority reside today. A Federal judge forced their removal from the U.S Terrorist Watchlist.

Today, the only thing the Iranian theocracy actually fears is the MEK, so the repression continues.

I spent weeks with the MEK, first at their Albanian Camp Ashraf 3 outside of Tirana, and then at their global headquarters in Paris. I spent hours interviewing many of their personnel. The MEK is essentially still a paramilitary operation.

The organization is run by females, as they show a future of equal rights for women within a tolerant Islam, not possible today in much of the Muslim world.

Their global satellite network beams a message of a free Iran into Iranian society. Their global fundraising operation across the Iranian diaspora is impressive.

The MEK has a ten-point plan to install democracy, freedom, equal rights, free markets, et cetera for the Persian people. You can read it at the end of this introduction.

At a minimum, the world needs to understand the true nature of the resistance to the regime in Iran, not what Western mockingbird media portrays.

The motto of the movement is — Pay the Price.

The MEK understands — freedom is not free.

Maryam Rajavi's Ten-Point Plan for Iran's Democratic Future

President-elect of the National Council of Resistance of Iran (NCRI) Maryam Rajavi's commitment to freedom and democracy in Iran has been outlined in her ten-point plan for the future of Iran. The NCRI is a coalition of more than 500 distinct Iranian opposition groups, including the People's Mujahedin Organization of Iran (MEK). The organization elected Maryam Rajavi as its leader, she runs the democratic Iranian government in exile.

Maryam Rajavi's ten-point plan for a brighter Iranian future

Maryam Rajavi's ten-point plan outlines the NCRI's vision for Iran following the end of the clerical rule. It serves as a roadmap for a new era of democratic rule, with the NCRI and Maryam Rajavi as the head of a tolerant democratic government.

Universal Suffrage

The first point of the plan asserts the NCRI's commitment to free and fair democratic elections. Legitimacy is earnt at the ballot box, and in a democratic Iran, the NCRI would hold fair elections with universal suffrage, granting every Iranian citizen a vote.

Political Freedom

The NCRI is committed to political freedom. Under its government, citizens would have the political freedom to create political parties, the media would be free of censorship, and all individuals would enjoy unrestricted access to the internet.

The Abolition of the Death Penalty

The NCRI and Maryam Rajavi oppose the use of the death penalty in all cases.

Secular Government

The NCRI is also determined to separate religion from government. Iran would become a place of religious freedom and pluralism, with followers of all religions welcome and free to practice their religious beliefs.

Equality

Maryam Rajavi and her NCRI government would uphold equality in all areas of Iranian society. Women would receive equal participation in political leadership, have the freedom to choose their clothing, their husbands, and be free to divorce.

Independent Judiciary

The NCRI is dedicated to the establishment of an independent judicial system. The accused would be considered innocent until proven guilty and have the right to legal counsel, defense in court, and a fair trial.

In Defense of Human Rights

Following the fall of the mullahs, the NCRI would uphold the Universal Declaration of Human Rights, eliminating discrimination against religious and ethnic minorities. The Iranian Kurdistan region will receive a plan of political autonomy, and all minority languages and cultures will receive the necessary protections.

A Market Economy

Maryam Rajavi and the NCRI seek to instate a market economy, with private property and investment. Investors will receive relevant protections and the NCRI will govern over a revitalized economy and environment.

The Pursuit of Peace

Iranian foreign policy will be based on the pursuit of peace and stability in the region. The NCRI will respect the UN Charter and seek peaceful coexistence with its international neighbors, both in the Middle East and beyond.

A Non-Nuclear Iran

Finally, the NCRI and Maryam Rajavi remain committed to establishing a non-nuclear Iran, free from weapons of mass destruction.

The Beginning

I had been to Ashraf 3 several times before, but marveled as it changed every time I passed through the gates. These people were very industrious and creative in perfecting a new home for themselves. The five men filtered into the conference room, and we enjoyed coffee and sweets before the conversation started.

They were elderly but not frail. There was a quiet confidence about them — a confidence that comes with starting, and surviving, a political revolution.

I had thought about attempting to write my own history of the MEK, but soon realized I could not do a better job than simply transcribing the spoken words of these wise men.

I typed fast as they spoke.

Early MEK member, Speaker #1:

"You have to understand the political and social circumstances at the time of the rise of the MEK. We've had a 120-year struggle for freedom. In 1906, we succeeded in a constitutional movement and elected Iran's first parliament — we were a constitutional monarchy. It was a progressive arrangement. Unfortunately, the British instituted a coup d'état and put their man in charge as they needed control. They installed Reza Khan ruler of Iran, an ex-army officer.

"Mohammed Mosaddeq was elected a member of parliament in Iran, the Majlis, the fifth parliament [after an already lengthy political career]. Mosaddeq opposed Reza Khan as king. Mosaddeq was imprisoned and exiled for some time. On October 31st of 1925, Khan put in place harsh repressive measures eliminating freedoms that had been previously given. In 1931 he passed a law — this is how we ended up in prison.

"During WWII, the allies met in Iran and decided to put Reza Khan in exile. They installed his son as the new shah of Iran. There was an open political environment during the change, and the people thrived. Mosaddeq was freed and became active in parliament; he had the most votes. Also, the Tudeh Party was very active in Iran; it was a mouthpiece of the Soviet KGB.

"One particular Mosaddeq initiative was to take back oil concessions that had been given to the British regarding Iranian energy resources in the south. In the north, the Tudeh Party and the Soviet Union were pressuring Iran to give concessions. One of the most important communists was Ja'far Pishevari, who formed a communist government in the north.

"Mosaddeq opposed communists; his new motto was 'negative balance.' Neither British nor Soviet influence was to be tolerated. It was quite a progressive model and wildly popular among Iranians, whose wealth benefited from this policy. Mosaddeq kicked out the British and nationalized Iranian oil. He went to the United Nations, The Hague, and won. Mosaddeq was revered by millions of Iranians.

"In 1952, the Shah dismissed Mosaddeq from being Prime Minister; there was a national uprising in support of Mosaddeq. A public backlash forced him back into the Prime Minister position. The Shah could not challenge Mosaddeq. He told the Shah, "You are only a figurehead, you have no role in running the government. This is where the United States begins its involvement in Iranian politics. To this day, it is a very important juncture.

"In 1953, a coup was organized by the CIA and MI6 with the collusion of the royal court, and clerics, including Abol-Ghasem Kashani. The coup brought down Dr. Mosaddeq. At this critical juncture, the United States, allied with reactionary clerics and the monarchial dictatorship, arrested Mosaddeq. His foreign minister, Dr. Hossein Fatemi, was executed by the Shah. All media was banned, and the progressive atmosphere was ended. Amir Mokhtar Karimpour Shirazi, a publisher, journalist, and virulently anti-Shah, was arrested and burned. The Shah's sister Ashraf ordered him to be burned to death.

"The Shah then formed the SAVAK, the hated secret police, and Iran became a police state after the coup d'état. This led to the suppression of the Iranian people. This demoralized Iranians. Seven years later, John F. Kennedy was elected president in the United States. This led to a slight opening in Iran in the political environment. The Iranian National Front, Mosaddeq's political party, was revived. Another movement, the National Movement of Iran, under Mehdi Bazargan, who later became prime minister under Khomeini, led this political movement, and was the reason for new freedoms.

"The CIA then analyzed that if there were no reforms, there would be another revolution, especially since the landowners had power within the royal court. The slogan of the National Movement of Iran was, "Monarchy yes, but constitution." The Shah was to be a figurehead.

"After a short while, many others were arrested and received maximum punishment. The SAVAK became omnipresent, suppressing any form of political activity. On June 5th, 1963, there was a major uprising nationwide, which the Shah brutally suppressed. He closed newspapers; many intellectuals were arrested. There was despair and hopelessness in Iranian society. If you read the poetry from this time, you will see the sense of despair. The Shah arrested Mohammad Hanifnejad and Saeid Mohsen, who were two of the initial founders of the MEK. Mohammad Hanifnejad always asked one question — why was the nationalist movement defeated? He spent his entire days going to people to find out why the movement failed and came to the conclusion that the Shah had closed down all avenues of peaceful activity in Iran. There was only one party in Iran — the Resurgence Party. Anyone who didn't like this could leave Iran. With the lack of freedoms, anyone who wanted to wage political opposition had to find out how this could be done.

"Ali-Asghar Badizadegan was also one of the founders of the MEK. They were all university grads. Badizadegan was an assistant professor, highly educated, and had tremendous knowledge of world history. In 1965, the three of them founded the MEK. Their first objective was to create an organization which would be qualified to wage an internal struggle against the Shah. Because of an extreme sense of responsibility, no name was given to the MEK. It had no name for a reason — if you gave it a name and were arrested, it would lead to people being demoralized. They didn't name the original movement. The most distinctive feature of the MEK is its ideology; it delved into Islamic teachings, the main sources for the religion — the Quran, and the Nahj al-Balagha [the road to eloquence] collection of sayings and writings of the first Shiite Imam Ali. By relying on these two sources, they arrived at the true essence of Islam and a message of shedding the reactionary interpretations of Islam that had been there for the past fourteen hundred years. In reading, they discovered several key tenants — one was [that] each and every human being and only him have the right to determine their way of living, and no one can compel them to choose a certain path in their lives. Even now, fifty-four years later, anyone who wishes to join the MEK must do so on his or her volition; they have to make that decision.

"The second point is that social evolution is an ongoing process, and we must adapt ourselves to the trend of social evolution or we will be left behind. Number three — the coming of the prophets was to establish social justice in certain societies, and they extracted from Islam two main messages of freedom and social justice — two unalienable principles. This includes gender equality, which is the main foundation of this ideology. Because the Shah could not reject or disparage the MEK founder's understanding of Islam, the Shah coined the term 'The Islamic Marxists.' This is where the source of Marxist labels comes from. In a general sense, one cannot redistribute, but the emphasis should be on giving maximum assistance to the impoverished — the poor, the deprived. Economic policies should address their needs. For example, there were lots of landowners, but those who work on the land, they should reap the benefits of their labor. This is how they presented their ideas, goals... This is how people joined.

"In 1966, Massoud Rajavi was among the founder of a tailors syndicate in Iran. In 1967, during parliamentary elections, SAVAK came to him and said [he] must mobilize tailors to vote for the Resurgence Party, the Shah's party. He rejected their urging. He regretted founding something that SAVAK could use. For two years, he was searching to find a movement to struggle against the Shah. Ultimately, he joined the MEK, becoming a member in 1969. He began to study several fields — Iranian history; different movements around the world in the 1960s: sociology, economics [and] economic theory; and began reading the Quran and other books with a different perspective. He had different teams working on different issues. For six years, he engaged in studies underground; nobody knew. This six-year period of study was very positive for the movement. It was also negative in the sense that SAVAK had not arrested them. They were very inexperienced in SAVAK's modus operandi in surveilling the opposition to the regime. SAVAK had become far more sophisticated in identifying dissidents. The MEK was clueless [as] to how it operated.

"On August 23, 1971, SAVAK launched raids against our homes [and] arrested many of our leaders and members in a two-month wave of arrests until the 23rd of October. It was a major blow to the movement. Eighty-five percent of our cadre were arrested. All the members of the central committee were arrested —

twelve members. When arrested, they began to discuss amongst themselves: why was SAVAK so successful? The answer was to evaluate what happened that allowed the arrests. At one point, all were put in one room — except for the founder, Mohammad Hanifnejad. They were able to send out of prison to the remaining members an analysis of failure, and devised a plan which succeeded in helping Reza Rezaei (central committee member) escape and reconstitute the organization. He had all the information that was gained, which was important in reviving the movement outside of prison. After that was over, the leaders of the MEK began to write their defense to present at the Shah's military tribunals later on.

"One of the most comprehensive defenses presented at the tribunal was by Massoud Rajavi. Another was by Saeid Mohsen. Their lengthy statements of defense were read out and have become part of the history of the anti-Shah struggle. SAVAK focused extensively on breaking Mohammad Hanifnejad. They put three conditions before him that, if he accepted, he would not be executed. The first was to say that armed struggle was a mistake. The second, to say that Islam is the enemy of Marxism. The third was that Iraq was giving financial assistance. Hanifnejad was not about to compromise; it was obvious he would be executed.

"SAVAK was looking to make the opposition movements enemies of each other — the other movement being the Marxist Fedayin. The three founders were executed on May 25, 1972, plus two other central committee members. This created a tremendous backlash. They were shot by firing squad. So many young men and women joined the MEK that we couldn't take them all. University protests in support of the MEK exploded; people provided a lot of support to the movement. The MEK was unable to take advantage of all the offers at the time. This demonstrated that the ideology of Islam and the policies of the Shah had tremendous resonance within society. Other groups did not have such sympathy, or Islamic orientation. All five of us here speaking were arrested and put in different prisons.

"All of the central committee members blamed themselves for the work of the organization. They took responsibility to let others get off easy, so many members were released as senior members took the blame. In the central committee, eleven of the twelve decided to take responsibility, but Reza Rezaei said he had no role. The others told him to pretend he was not a hardcore revolutionary.

"Reza had an older brother named Ahmed. Reza suggested to the SAVAK, perhaps he could help capture Ahmed. When the families would visit, Reza told his family about the plan and to please tell Ahmed to implement it. Reza told SAVAK about a public bath location where Ahmed takes a bath. Reza told them he had to go in alone or they will not trust. The SAVAK stopped at the door, but the bathhouse had a back door. The MEK members escaped, including Reza. The agents waited two hours and he did not come back. The bathhouse is still there on Bouzarjomehri Street in Tehran.

Speaker #5 added something at this point:

"The escape was extremely important. It created a situation to desensitize SAVAK about Reza. When all were arrested, the other said they 'kicked out a SAVAK agent.' Families would be conduits to send [or] take information. Massoud Rajavi had also recruited several younger people... all three were arrested on August 23, 1971. However, three were released, as Massoud had developed a plan. He had placed an advertisement in the local paper saying he was accepting students to teach English. Their names were Mohammad-rez Khansari, Hashmand Khameneh, and Mostafa Malayen. SAVAK bought the paper to confirm."

Speaker #1:

"Another point — after the revolution, fast forward to the first parliamentary/presidential election in 1980. I was the campaign chief for the MEK during both elections.

"When Khomeini came to power, our analysis of the situation was this: there were two points of view. The first view was that the main focus of the election should be respect for freedom in Iran and the challenge of democratic freedom for reactionaries that monopolized every aspect of life, including power. The second opinion was shared by Khomeini, the Tudeh Party, and some smaller Muslim groups. This was that there was a danger in the revolution as liberals were conduits for the return of U.S. imperialism to Iran. The mullahs said the anti-American struggle should take precedence. Khomeini was a dark genius who had created the negative impression that people blamed the U.S. for the Shah.

Khomeini was smart... he used anti-American sentiment to consolidate his base of power and eliminate the opposition as American stooges. The Soviets had interest in this and supported the Tudeh Party in Iran. *This is an extremely important point in Iran — why did the MEK and Khomeini oppose each other?* The fight with Khomeini was only over the issue of freedom. This had resonance within society as that is what people wanted — freedom. The intellectuals were particularly supportive of this policy.

"On January 5th, 1980, Massoud Rajavi announced his candidacy for president. It was time to unify the democratic, liberal forces around Rajavi's platform. He formed local councils to address issues in every sector of society — independence, territorial integrity, the people's sovereignty, complete freedom of political parties, free speech of opinion, of the media, respect for Iranian ethnic minorities, gender equality in economic and social arenas and there would be no distinction between Sunnis and Shiites. There would be equality among all denominations. The peasants would have ownership of land, and workers would have ownership of their work. This was the plan Rajavi put forth, an alternative to what Khomeini had presented.

"The campaign lasted ten days. Rajavi was so popular that Khomeini issued a fatwa nullifying his candidacy as president, even though he said he would not interfere. Before the announcement, Rajavi went to see the acting minister of the interior, Rafsanjani. Rajavi had boycotted the assembly of clerics where they instituted the absolute rule of the clergy, the valayat-e faqih. The MEK said this was undemocratic and boycotted the meeting. The

MEK did not vote for the constitution. Rafsanjani said he welcomed the MEK to take part in the elections, however. There was a tremendous groundswell across the nation for Rajavi and his platform. On the 20th of January, 1980, Khomeini issued a fatwa stating those who did not vote for the constitution cannot run for president. This was just before the elections. Another prominent political prisoner, Shokrollah Paknejad — the Shah referred to him as a left-leaning activist — belonged to a different political party. He went to Iranian Kurdistan and returned. He told us he wanted to meet Rajavi and that all Kurdish parties will vote for Rajavi. He was also in contact with Armenians, Jews, Baluchis, Turkman, and Arabs. He met Rajavi, and based on my calculations, Rajavi had ten million votes because of it. The journalist Eric Rouleau, writing for Lemond newspaper in France, an advisor to Mitterand, wrote on the 29th of January, 1980, that if Imam Khomeini had not vetoed Rajavi's candidacy, he would have secured millions of votes because he was enjoying the support of ethnic and religious minorities due to his support for equal rights and autonomy. He also had a major portion of women and young people in his camp because he rejected the reactionary clerical rule. The presidency would have been his.

"During the first parliamentary elections, we formed a council with the MEK and liberal progressive groups, including the National Democratic Front, to select candidates. The council was to nominate progressive candidates for parliament. In an official announcement by the government, the interior ministry, the MEK had secured 25% of votes nationwide. Rajavi garnered 531k votes in Tehran. He was running for parliament. You would imagine you would get at least one member of parliament elected, but none were allowed by the mullahs.

"During the elections, Rajavi had meetings in cities where hundreds of thousands of supporters would show up in East Azerbaijan, along the Caspian Sea. Within the ruling elite, there was a weak trend of those who were liberal-minded. We tried to attract them to the MEK against the mullahs; we tried to make sure there was no conflict and to move the process along as peacefully as possible. For example, even the Prime Minister said people should support the MEK.

"On June 15, 1980, there was a major rally in Tehran. Club-wielding thugs attacked the rally and beat up people. Even Khomeini's son and thirty members of parliament asked why the government attacked without permission?

"On June 25, 1980, Khomeini spoke. He said the enemy is not the USSR, not the US — the enemy is the MEK. They are hypocrites, worse than infidels. Our singular focus from February 1979 to June 1981 was to try and prevent the process from turning violent and to secure a peaceful political process; and the tendency, however weak, from the ruling apparatus towards the democratic forces to ensure freedoms in Iran were respected, to prevent the consolidation of power under Khomeini. But he managed to do it anyway.

"We want to emphasize — the democratic process remains alive. Rajavi rallied to retain rights in the face of regime repression in front of hundreds of thousands, and we will fight to uphold

freedom... In the Muslim movement, freedom is essential to ensure and safeguard and prolong humanity."

***

Speaker #2:

"I became a member of the MEK in 1969. I have a Bachelor of
Science in business and industrial engineering from Tehran. I was
an expert at the Iranian Ministry of Economy. At that time, I became a member of the MEK; myself, and my younger brother Ali,
and my sister were at Ashraf as members of the MEK. My younger
sister and her husband were killed when the IRCG attacked our
home in Tehran in August of 1982.

"When I was young, tenth to twelfth grade, I took part in meeting of the National Front, from '60 to '62. In 1962, the Shah dis-
solved all political parties. In 1963, he massacred protesters from
different Iranian cities. This is why I was attracted to the MEK. I
was a religious intellectual, from the lower middle class, watching
the impoverishment of the Iranian people in a wealthy oil country. The other factor was the character of the founders of the MEK.
After the 1953 coup, the leaders of the Tudeh Party were arrested.
There was distrust in Iranian society. There was an atmosphere of
repression and fear. It was difficult to trust anyone. What attracted me to the MEK was when I met Mohammad Hanifnejad
and other central committee members on May 25, 1972. I was attracted to their sincerity, to their honesty, selflessness; they didn't
want to do anything for themselves. They devoted their entire
lives to the improvement of the Iranian people and freedom. The

third factor was their progressive view of Islam... a democratic Islam, intertwined with freedom.

"What I want to mention now, before the revolution — why, after so many years of struggle against the Shah and his influence in the universities, why did Khomeini come to power as the mullah in Najaf?

"In September of 1971, everyone was arrested. In fact, it again started inside Evin Prison, when we were all arrested... the famous notorious torture. But it was important to keep communication with each other. For example, for the Reza escape, it was my responsibility for his escape. He came out of the cell for fresh air. There was a small yard and windows for each cell. For Reza, the window was near the ceiling and very small. In the courtyard, we noticed the face of Reza. Somehow, he had reached that window. He couldn't talk... all of the guards were there. But with sign language and body language, we knew what was happening.

"One of the people who tried communication was Rajavi, from inside the prison. He was in bad condition. We managed to see him after six months. He had lost 20kg because of torture. They flogged the soles of his feet. They flogged his face, his head, and back. He was bleeding in his stomach."

Speaker #5:

"The guards at Evin said, 'If you don't give information, you will be tortured like Rajavi.'"

Speaker #2:

"They used metal cables and electricity, which were excruciating. They would take off the flesh... the soles of your feet had blisters and they would burst. They would put sharp objects into the wounds and hit them. Another man could not sit upright and developed a hunchback due to torture. They would burn your flesh with the iron. For treatment, one man had to get a skin graft to his leg and back. Rajavi had terrible headaches and pain in his body. At the same time, he was writing about political achievements and strategy for the PMOI. He had such bad headaches, he had to put handkerchief around his head to cure. Everything had to be written down. When transferred to other prisons, he would write on cigarette papers. They were handed off and copied. They would steal pens during interrogations and hide in the body, so not to be found during a search. They would pass to the family.

"One guy was released one month before everyone else. He would go to the prisons to meet with them, his brother and Rajavi. He used to bring cigarettes. He would pass packs of cigarettes back and forth with notes inside. Police would check and pass on. After a six-year struggle going on outside and inside the prisons, scripts of their defense smuggled outside prisons by prisoners, people in society realized the organization existed. A progressive, Islamic organization existed against the Shah, and it encouraged young intellectuals to join us as well. The PMOI moved Islamic to society as part of their struggle for freedom. This is how the MEK was welcomed.

"They first started to support the MEK in the universities. These places were known as a bastion of freedom. Also, a concentration of Iranian students outside the U.S. started to support the MEK. Other elements, including members of families inside prison, became active in disseminating the goals of the MEK. They disclosed the way the torture happened. This went deep inside society. In 1976, President Jimmy Carter announced his human rights priorities. This pressured the Shah. He quit the torture and executions. That made people have the right to have their voices heard. The protests echoed the voice of the MEK inside the prisons. All small protests developed into democratic protests by millions of people on the street.

"So why did Khomeini come to power? Because Khomeini was the biggest thief of the century. The revolution was started by progressives; he pocketed the revolution. He could do it through the network of the mullahs, as they were free and not inside the prisons. Khomeini did nothing during the revolution. The revolution started and then Khomeini came on the scene. After that, all the different social strata joined the movement. Khomeini wrote a message to the mullahs... Don't worry, they have not been harmed... come out and talk... to the mullahs. He also abused the absence of the progressive leaders who were inside the prisons until the fall of the Shah.

"Then Khomeini went to Paris in May of 1978 and did the Le Monde interview — which the BBC broadcasted — supporting the mullahs, the clerics who went to the British embassy for past protests. The clerics always had connections with the British government. The British told the U.S. press the MEK was Marxist and would go with the Soviets. The BBC was in the tank for the mullahs. They have a long history — the English and the mullahs. The English banked on the mullahs for influence over Iranian society. The Anglo-American Oil Company... it was about money, lots of money. Jack Straw was very close to the mullahs and put us on the terrorist list. The U.K. propped up Khomeini in Paris, and in Najaf.

"The U.S. pushed land reform under the Shah away from the feudal system. With JFK, we moved away from the British... the mullahs were opposed to this... these were anti-reactionary reforms.

"In 1978, whatever reforms the Shah did, he could not stop the movement. He changed ministers, et cetera. Ambassador Sullivan from the U.S. and the British ambassador met with the Shah and said the Shah was demoralized. They said the Shah could not remain in power anymore. Khomeini moved to Paris; was in touch with the U.S. government, also the French government, and made hollow promises to the U.S. and France. The U.S. wanted assurances from Khomeini that U.S. interests would not be touched. The U.S. prevented the Iranian army from moving against Khomeini. 'Do not attempt a coup'... that is how the revolution was derailed. U.S. policy has screwed up the country... let the people decide. We asked why Khomeini didn't support the MEK; he said because of their social base. They will come to power instead of the mullahs. Khomeini took over.

"The Shah invented the term 'Islamic Marxism' against the MEK. The Shah commuted Rajavi's sentence to life. The Shah was later disappointed he did not execute Rajavi. He knew he had to isolate and put him in solitary confinement. I saw documents from SAVAK to the Shah. They said Rajavi is preventing other prisoners from repenting. He told the mullahs to say the MEK are Islamic Marxists.

"The narrative is that Khomeini led the revolution and was the rightful leader. This was NOT the case. Many groups, poets, intellectuals, students, et cetera, opposed the Shah. But all the leaders were executed or were in prison. When the transfer of power came, Khomeini stepped into it.

"In the Paris meetings, Bani Sadr and other U.S. Iranians manipulated them for liberal democracy. The clerical establishment remained intact during the revolution. The clerics were getting money from the Shah. Khomeini played the anti-communist card. There was apprehension within the U.S. intelligence movement over the MEK. The only force who could take over were the mullahs. They had all the mosques; Khomeini emerged as the de facto leader of the revolution.

"The Iranian people had no idea who would replace the Shah."

***

Speaker #5:

"In October of 1966, Rajavi came to know Mousa Khiabani, who later became the MEK's number two in command. Both were students of science at Tehran University. He was very upset about the Shah and the repressive society, and active against it. Mousa

asked Rajavi privately; Rajavi welcomed the opportunity to re-
cruit but did not tell him about the MEK, for nine months. He
would have Mousa read books, and make reports back and forth.
Only when he became assured that he consciously had chosen to
follow this path, did he tell him in September of 1967 about the
MEK. Rajavi was very careful that everyone was recruited voluntarily. After the attacks by the SAVAK, the conclusion was you
have to create something new that did not exist before to go
against the Shah... nothing existed.

"The opposition needed strategy... wanted an organization
who were professional, and dedicated to their work. Rajavi had
formulated this strategy for six years. He wanted the mindset to
be: do everything for others, not for yourself. For example, Rajavi
went hiking together often with MEK members... he was out in
the mountains one day when he saw four others ahead. He fig-
ured they were MEK, but he did not know. They came to a place
where they could not go anymore, where it was very dangerous.
One of the four said, 'I have a way to go down,' and he fashioned
a rope with shawls and showed the others how to get down. It
worked and all followed. Rajavi didn't know who he was until
Rajavi was arrested by SAVAK. Two months later, after torture,
two people came up to Rajavi and put his feet in warm water and
gave him a massage. One of them was the person who had
showed them the way down from the mountain. Rajavi pushed
putting your lives on the line to save each other. This is the basis
of MEK longevity. Everyone does so out of his own decision.

"My first rendezvous with a superior was a meeting in a small
one-room apartment. I later found out it was Mohammad

Hanifnejad. I noticed he was very sincere, friendly, and that is what attracted him to the MEK. This was the first lesson — he said, if you look at the world, at inception, it was just shapeless hydrogen, then with evolution, matter developed, then chemicals, then life, then animals, and humans are at the pinnacle. This explains when I chose the MEK, I permanently abandoned returning to life as usual. No secrets were being divulged. When eighty percent were arrested by SAVAK, if any of them had cooperated, everyone else would have been arrested. But none were arrested. We were arrested during an operation, not due to information being released. The training created people who were very resistant and committed to the cause.

"On June 25th, the regime said all security forces would focus on identifying and arresting MEK in Iran. The government said the MEK can mobilize 500,000 people, and engaged in a massive surveillance operation. They identified homes; when they arrested people, they would execute them. They would post pictures of the bodies and ask families to come identify them. They would attack homes and set them on fire. They used RPGs, helicopter gunships. In February of 1982, many safe houses were attacked. Khiabani, the second in command, his wife, and eighteen others were killed in northern Tehran. Then, in August of '82, many safe houses were attacked. They again used RPGs, heavy machine guns, opened fire, setting the houses on fire; they wanted to liquidate. In August of that year, we lost sixty people; the MEK was the second-largest party in Iran. Many members should have made parliament, but not even one person. We tried to expose all the rigging and the fraud. We forced the regime to set up a debate to discuss election fraud.

"Rhouhani was the Islamic Party representative and Rajavi was opposing him in the debate. He was presenting documents on rigging and Rhouhani had nothing to say... so he offered a bigger lie — the reason you didn't win is because lies in newspapers that mullahs are reactionaries. Rajavi said, you have written this, and the newspaper is in front of you... the article said some members were reactionary. His face turned white, as he knew he had lied.

***

Speaker #3:

"I knew about the MEK in 1971. I was a student. At the time, people were thinking, what can be done to counter the Shah? I had been arrested twice for distributing leaflets. When I read the defense of the MEK leaders on TV, I learned about the MEK. Fedayin had engaged in armed resistance; while we had sympathized, we also felt Marxism was not fulfilling. When we heard the MEK defense, they were Muslim. We came to realize a Muslim group was fighting against the regime. It was a source of encouragement and hope that an Islamic alternative existed. Before this, we were at a crossroads. Traditional Islam was the spokesman of the mullahs. On the other hand, the Marxists were internationally recognized, as there were other countries leading the revolution, and this was attractive to some Iranian intellectuals. With the realization the MEK did exist, we had found what we wanted. They would be responsive to what we wanted to achieve. In many respects, you cannot separate religion from society, even under the Shah. He said he was a shadow of God on Earth. From a cultural perspective, the king god had resonance; many believed God was the key to society, good and bad selection. This includes why the mullahs were in bed with the Shah; for the mullahs, the conflict was not with the Shah but with those who believe in God. Many men said this is not a paradigm where we can work... this marked the difference between the mullahs and MEK Islam.

"Marxism rejects religion. The MEK was independent-minded. The MEK wanted democratic Islam. The emblem of the sickle should represent defending the individual's rights. The star was from the Quran, and referred to those who lead and give their lives for the struggle. The MEK was cognizant of the link between Iranian culture and Marxism. We chose democratic Islam as an ideology. The MEK swam against the current by defining Islam as they saw it.

"Also political independence. The interest of the Iranian people was the priority and not the interests of foreign powers. Independence became very prominent in society as a whole. Marxism became isolated in Iran, due to the betrayal of the Tudeh Party.

"The cornerstone of MEK ideology was distance from the reactionary mullahs of Islam. The mullahs drew their credibility originally from the MEK. The mayor of Tehran's brother was MEK. Even early on, the mullahs supported the MEK. It goes to show how ridiculous the narrative is that the MEK has no support inside Iran.

"I was in prison four years before the regime change. I became aware of a coup d'état of Marxists within the MEK, people who launched the coup engaged in violent tactics, killing remaining MEK leaders and those who did not become Marxist. In order to cover up what they had done, they killed six Americans. These Americans were killed by Marxists. They usurped the leadership due to the absence of leadership — we were in prison. This was a shock to Iranian society who believed in the MEK.

"MEK activists at UCLA, men who became pacified, or even Marxists, destroyed the confederation of students at that time; the coup d'état gave justification to what the mullahs had been saying, that maybe the Shah was right. This unleashed reactionary Islam back on Iran. I served the interests of the Shah.

"Two years later, people came to the street which led to the overthrow of the Shah. Khomeini used the term Islamic Marxists and threatened to unleash the army.

"The coup made mobilization of supporters impossible for us. My first statement after leaving prison was to oppose the opportunistic views of the mullahs and acknowledge freedom.

"We set up offices for the MEK across the cities of Iran. Many people wanted to join, and we printed a questionnaire. We organized lessons on the MEK's goals, strategies, our belief in democratic Islam. The MEK was the dominant force in the universities.

***

Speaker #4:

"I was a senior at Sharif University of Technology; it was the MIT of Iran. Sharif was murdered by opportunists and his name put on the school. The mullahs can't change it.

"My religious beliefs contradicted the struggle against the Shah. Marxism was a natural venue, but I saw it as an opportunity to look for a third way. I was introduced to the MEK and found what I was looking for in 1970. I was arrested in 1972 by the SAVAK police, who had formed a committee against sabotage. I was tortured for four months, then transferred to Qasr Prison and sentenced to death for acting against national security. For twenty-two years I witnessed tortured... the Apollo torture method, where a metal hood was put on your head, they tied up your arms and feet, the scream would echo within the hood on your head. I saw how many women were tortured. The SAVAK was angry at MEK influence on society.

"After torture, I was transferred to the general ward and met with other prisoners. Prison became the center of activity. The MEK grew inside the prisons; our prisoner population grew. The movement grew. Many pro-MEK students were arrested and brought to prison during the Nixon visit. The Shah instructed them to increase the pressure on prisoners. In 1974, the prison guards attacked the prisoners; things got out of control. The SAVAK appealed to the prison population to help control. They tried to calm the tense environment. The MEK used the opportunity to train prisoners to become MEK activists outside. The regime would give long sentences to keep prisoners in prison, even for small offenses. The real MEK was being built within the prisons. Books were written against what the Marxists had written. When released, because prisoners came from different cities, the MEK was able to organize quickly with the prisoner release. Rajavi was released ten days before Khomeini came back to Iran.

"The MEK was afraid the Shad would kill Rajavi and other senior members at that time before the Shah fell. Khomeini was not happy about the release of political prisoners. People gathered around the prison until the prisoners were released. The military blows of the Shah, and the coup d'état against the movement, gave us a chance to rebuild the movement. We organized a national movement in every city after the fall of the Shah. Two days after the revolution, we were in 127 cities, where supporters and sympathizers came. Many young people joined the MEK — every sector of Iranian society, including the traders' guild in the bazaar. Many members were executed for giving support to the MEK. Some had associations with Muslim workers, women and men. They had a newspaper called the Cry of the Shantytown Dwellers. Also, an association of cadets among the military.

"The U.S. Embassy hostage-taking was a way... after the Iran-Iraq War, for Khomeini to consolidate power. He betrayed every promise he made in Paris, and enshrined the rule of the clerics. There was no constitutional monarchy. On June 20th, the regime dismissed Bani Sadr. The MEK called for protest and had to go underground within twenty-four hours; there were thousands of arrests and thousands of executions.

"Rajavi announced, on July 21st, the organization of the National Council for Resistance in Iran, the NCRI, and the organization sent Rajavi to Paris. Many military helped Rajavi get out of Iran. The regime was shocked."

***

The moderator of the session then spoke up, heralding the arrival of lunch. But he wanted to make one thing clear: "There was nothing about liberated Islam in writing or social proxy in the beginning of the mullah's reign; a significant part of Iranian history has been created and perverted, even eliminated, by the regime. This is important to note."

At that point, we ended the session and subsequently enjoyed a fabulous meal of Iranian cuisine.

The Real Feasts

This day I spent with the female leaders and soldiers of the MEK. Their stories were heartbreaking and inspiring, and I listened with awe. The MEK is the most "equal rights" organization I have ever come across.

Western feminists should be ashamed of themselves. These are the real feminists — those who use their feminine strength to fight, in their own way, against repression.

Speaker #1:

"I was involved with the MEK since the early days of the Shah at Sharif University in Tehran. I joined the MEK in 1976, but I understood about the MEK since early '71 when the founders were arrested. I learned by reading their defense and found it attractive.

"Once I joined, that is all I did — 24/7. I left university and went underground, became intimately involved in the movement as a whole. I saw the important role women had then, and now, and how they assumed positions of responsibility. The reality with this dictatorship is that women will not enjoy any kind of promotion or advance unless they engage in the struggle against dictatorship... no movement will be successful unless women play a prominent role against it. We needed organized opposition to lead the movement.

"Women faced a lot of obstacles to be active in traditional society and in political activity. Of course, this was because of reactionary Islam. These obstacles had shackled women; this continued until the MEK was formed. The MEK was attractive because it espoused a modern Islam and was trying to bring freedom. In 1971, the MEK became known... intellectually and within families... and understood the cultural sensitivity.

"There were a few others with Marxist tendencies... The Muslim part of the MEK opened the door for women to become active. Fatimeh, our main teacher, joined in 1970 and, in '74, went underground. She was killed under torture march in 1954. This broke taboo weakness and despair among women of the anti-Shah movement. She became a symbol of resistance for women in Iran. Her martyrdom showed an independent woman who can resist torture, and give the ultimate sacrifice. I knew her personally. When I saw her struggle, I said — I can do it, women can endure much. Behjat Tiftakchi also had tremendous character; she was killed under the Shah's regime. Ashraf Rabiei married Massoud Rajavi. She was also at Sharif University. She had an appealing character, was full of love, had many former friends, and was a very strong person. She was arrested several times. Upon release was the last time she went underground. She was released three weeks before the fall of the Shah, and killed when Khomeini attacked her house in 1982."

Speaker #2:

"I was born into a wealthy family, religious, highly cultured and politically aware. My father was a scientist, researcher, publisher, and author. Because of traditional society in Iran, I had no capacity to become politically active until the arrest of the leadership of the MEK when I came to know about the organization. SAVAK found out about my ties to these men. At fifteen years old, I found myself in a big university in prison, a university on perseverance, sacrifice, struggle; I saw many role models, one hundred women were political prisoners. Despite many types of torture, they kept high morale, were extremely capable, political, and at the same time humble, compassionate... despite their wounds. They were the first to exercise, boost morale. "After flogging soles of their feet, being beat by torturers, their feet would get infected. Some died of infection in the blood. They would pull nails, feet and fingers.

"After the fall of the Shah, it became much more brutal. Many were wounded when arrested. They drove sharp objects into the wounds. Massoumeh Shadmani, called Mother Kabiri, they flogged her feet.

"She was arrested by SAVAK in '81 for her support for the MEK. She was tortured so severely by the mullahs that all the flesh was gone from her feet. Below the feet, there was no flesh. Prisoners saw the head of Evin Prison, Asadollah Ladjevardi, kill her with a head shot. Glasses would not stay on her face, as she lost so much weight.

"Ashraf Ahadi, another hero, had been arrested with her toddler, also a prisoner under the Shah. She was imprisoned 4 years, and arrested again by Khomeini, tortured and killed in the massacre in 1988.

"Some others survived.

"I was sentenced to 5 years in prison, commuted to three years, and released."

Speaker #3:

"I was born in a traditional family; my older brother Mustafa was a member of the MEK. I went to high schools run by Islamic scholars. Because of the role of Mustafa and his presence in our household, and influence, he became [known] to families of MEK in prison. My brother became a role model and was executed. I had a wealthy family; father was opposed to MEK as a traditional family, but mother was okay with it. My family really liked Mustafa. He was a very ethical person, distinct from others, a lot of good memories; he was my hero.

"Mustafa was the third oldest, and my younger sister and I became very close after his arrest. For a long time, they refused to let us see him. After eight months, Mother saw him and began crying. She didn't recognize him. He told Mother she should not cry and said, 'resist, don't show weakness.' It was a long way, but Mother would go there every day with many other families. That way, all the families got to know each other. The goal was to achieve freedom from all political prisons and become an organization to let people know what prisoners to look for. We would find out which prisoner was being tortured, denied food, and we would have a small protest with other family members of the prisoner. Security forces arrived and political prisoners disbursed, escaped the scene.

"This allowed us to break out of the imposed traditional environment, break the grip of restrictions and build a quasi-organizational structure. We wrote graffiti, exchanged MEK books, prisoner messages, shared info from prison, vice versa on the news to and from prisons, who were expelled. We held protests in front of the prosecutor's office. We would partake in the trials in public, put tape recorders in prison; this meeting created a political environment inside and out of prison. We held a historic sit-in for one full month. We were not the last group. Because of our sit-in, the last group was released. This is how the role of women grew into a very prominent role in 1979. Some women took part in the military rebellion against the Shah."

Speaker #2:

"Under the Shah, there was no sexual abuse, none. During the Shah's time, women would get dates [fruit], as added nutrition. Under Khomeini, they knew no boundaries torturing women. The reason for the savagery against women — the MEK fights against misogyny. The mullahs think they are guardians of religion, but women have no rights; this is totally contrary to Islamic teachings. We had serious conflict with the mullahs on issues of women, issues of freedom. Women are totally free to do anything in the MEK's view. Because the mullahs want to impose their own rule, they exploit Islam, impose dictatorship and absolute rule of the jurisprudence. What women endured in the prisons of Khomeini is unprecedented anywhere in the world. They would extract blood of prisoners before execution, force woman prisoners to marry revolutionary guards the night before execution, gang rapes to break their resistance and character, torturing children and mothers in front of each other, husband and wife."

Speaker #1"

"In the West, feminism is only a political issue. The mullahs trample on their very principles in support of the regime. This is why the MEK appeal is so popular. The one thing is unalienable insistence of principles no matter what the cost; that in a nutshell is a struggle for freedom. The degree to which women have freedom to do what they want is a benchmark to how free a society is. From our perspective, judge only by the degree they take action against the regime in Iran. There is a tremendous face-off between the MEK and the regime in Iran; it does not recognize any rights for women except being dominated and owned by men. It comes from the depth of the reactionary and filthy outlook towards woman. An ideology that is based on freedom, creates opportunity for all human beings, men or women. Opportunities in this movement are equal footing with men in the movement as a whole."

Speaker #3:

"Before going to visit my brother, I read the Quran daily. In March of 1975, nine political prisoners were killed attempting to escape Evin Prison. Nobody believed it. Two thousand came to visit as my brother was one of the nine. In April 1975, Mustafa and another central committee member Kazem Zolanvar, and senior MEK members, along with seven leading members of the Fediyan organization, were shot by firing squad. This was a very important event in history of Shah's regime.

"The head torturer of the Shah lives in L.A. and admitted nine prisoners were executed, but justified it by saying they tried to escape.

"Resistance of MEK women in prison under the Shah, and activities of the families outside of prison across the country compelled a wide presence of women in the anti-Shah movement. Female political activity increased under the mullahs."

Speaker #4:

"Emotions are difficult to control when you hear the stories again. You cannot just hear it and let it go by. Get a copy of the confession of torturer from Ali [MEK guide during interviews]. In 1971, my older sister was at the University of Tehran. She was in contact with the MEK, and received the defense of the MEK in the courts. She read, and sent to me to introduce me to the ideals of the MEK. I was a high school student, of course thinking about the future. She knew I was looking for something, and introduced me to the ideals of the MEK. I was very enthusiastic — I found what I [was] looking for! One thing I knew for sure: I had to rebel against the status quo. I would share with my classmates, they would read, and it would inspire them tremendously. My sister was arrested in 1972. After release from prison in 1973, she continued the activities with MEK. She was underground, but was killed in 1976 in a clash with security forces in Tehran. People in prison became aware of her martyrdom and told us. She had a distinguished personality within the family; a lot of people were influenced by her. She was very kind, had tremendous love, and was very much opposed to gender discrimination. There should be no discrimination. She showed tremendous courage when engaging in her activities. People looked up to her very much. When my father heard, he said, 'Don't feel sorry for yourself; she chose the path she wanted to follow, and I'm proud of her that she did what she did.'

"We all talked about the Shah's time, but I want to make an important point about the Shah's time to the mullah's era. The expansion of the role of women in the struggle, what led to the role of women. Because of the repression under the Shah, once overthrown, women found the gates open to them to continue with political activity. We saw dramatic leaps when it came to women's role in the movement. There were two main factors — one, a relative degree of freedom with no Shah. Two, the MEK leaders were released from prison — came into society. In an interview with Kahan published in February 1979, one day before the fall of Shah's regime, he said an urgent issue is the issue of women. [NCRI President Elect] Mariam Rajavi emphasized — one of the most distinctive feature of the MEK s is widespread participation of women. I must congratulate women for such a big role. Of course, added to that, many classes within the organization are diametrically opposed to keeping women in the house; this led to training of a generation of women that became more and more wider spread and comprised women in every sector of Iranian society...high schools, university, workers, offices, teachers, etc. I was a teacher at the time and formed teacher's movement in the

MEK. Teachers would gather and share and disseminate ideals, teach during the day and political activity in the evening."

Speaker #5:

"Azam Haj Heidari was a teacher and active in teacher's organizations, participated in MEK election activities, was arrested several times, and worked with our own students. Students' families told me about it in advance. She continued activities and in 1981 was arrested. I got to know the MEK in 1973, at age seventeen, when again she was put on trial on Iranian state TV. They broadcast the trial. I was sympathetic to friends to the MEK: I hoped very much to be like them and fight for freedom. But because of the repression, and traditional culture in families, I did not have the opportunity to engage in political activities. But once it became public, we became familiar with MEK ideology and what they were trying to accomplish. Demonstrations against the Shah, we took part in all of them, broke the taboo participating in political and social activities and came in direct contact with the MEK after fall of the Shah. I got to know some senior figures in the MEK in the anti-Shah movement, and it paved for way for me to get engaged, attain what I wanted to obtain — I could rebel against the status quo and change the environment. The mullahs culture and outlook are for women to stay in the home and be housewives. My family was the same. My brother said he would give me anything I want if I didn't join the MEK. But I recognized the choice of either the veil or a hit on the head. So, I rejected everything my family offered and chose to join ranks of the MEK. In 1981, my brother went to security forces and informed on me. I was arrested by the mullahs. My friends had told me about the Shahs' prisons — and in Khomeini's prisons.

"Their aim with women was to break their character and human identity, force them to surrender to the mullahs' misogynist outlook. There were widespread arrests of female activists with the MEK. The first moment I entered, I saw women from all walks of life and ages. I also saw toddlers who couldn't yet walk, a lot of high school girls; eleven, thirteen, sixteen; a lot of pregnant women being tortured; students; physicians; teachers, like myself. What was very shocking to me, 2 by 3 meters, sixty to seventy female prisoners. The Warden of Evin — "I want to tell you something you will remember forever, if we had the possibility we would make solitary cells for each and every MEK prisoner so none of you could speak to one another because you are who you are when you are together.

"They tried to build solitary cells for the MEK. The eighth floor — we [were] taken there first and interrogated, tortured, executed. They called it a dormitory. They built cells in another prison, Qezel Hesar in Karaj, 40 kilometers west of Tehran. They built cells called 'the cage'... 150 centimeters by 50 centimeters. We were put in such cells for days and days and days... were prohibited [from] speaking to each other, even praying. All offenses, torture for that, whoever violated was sent to the cage. I was in one of those cells for eight months squatted. They hit us on the head and face and body with cables. The head of prison, called Davood Rahmani, who would say, 'This prison is for you hell on earth.' He said, 'this is doomsday, either confess or will keep you here until you die, decay and die.' There were absolutely no rights, no food, no water, no choice, not even a word. It was psychological torture. At midnight they would play tape recordings of women screaming while being tortured, or air radio broadcasts, propaganda, to demoralize, to doubt herself and what she had done. They would go to the cells, the ones confined to the cage to repent, there is no use for you to resist.

"But they failed utterly to break even one of us in those cages, they could not break our conviction or penetrate what was in our hearts. We did not doubt our paths even one iota, the more they tortured us, the more we demanded freedom... because of our perseverance, international pressure, they were forced to take us out of those cells.

"Each faction was trying to blame it on the other part of the IRGC, all of these torture methods. In 1971, there were press conferences at the UN every year. They spoke about all of this for three years in a row. A lot was written about this... forcing the regime to abandon the cage. The Shah's prison were different. They would hang women from the ceilings for several days on... there was widespread use of rape... or mock executions, for one week every day they took me to hills and lined us up for mock execution. It was 6:00 a.m. in snow, winter time. They would bring back by 6:00 p.m. to solitary 209. One time I was very cold, hypothermia, I heard someone trying to talk with Morse code and I was happy to speak to someone. I asked what her name was — Massomi Najar... Rajavi's sister, she was captured in a raid, husband killed, shot in jaw, tortured to death —older sister was killed by the Shah. She was pregnant, every day there was torture, they opened the door of cell and threw in a snake. She was tortured so much she could not walk. The snake came next to her, and she touched the head of snake. She told me this in Morse. The interrogator would see this reaction and she would be petting it. They felt that didn't affect her, so they took away the snake.

"They would take us for interrogation, put our feet into sack a full of roaches. They also built a series of solitary cells — called residential unit — and took many women for more than a year and exposed them to various forms of torture. Then they would bring them out. You are not allowed to talk to anyone. If you talk to anyone we will take you to execution. Many of the women in the residential units became insane, because of torture, psychological abuse. One woman I know, Farzaneh Amooiee, had a very young child, another one master's degree in physics. She was creative and had new ideas, always teaching other women in prison. She went insane. The head of the prison said, 'All of you will go crazy. We will make sure none of you will survive, none of you will leave.' This was the residential unit meaning. For them the tortures against women were limitless.

"A sixteen-year-old girl was arrested for sympathy to the MEK and put in solitary ward 311 Evin Prison.

"She was tortured so much all her body had deep scars. They would flog more on wounds and return her. They beat her so much and she would resist so much they would grow desperate and tired of beating her. One torturer would get tired and hand her over to another. Begging her to at least give her name and they wouldn't execute but she wouldn't and they took her to cell and the next morning realized she had died.

"Another example of torture under Khomeini... my colleague Shahala had two children, one son and one daughter. Her husband was an official in the regime. She had everything you could ask for. If she wanted to live a simple life, no problem. But she had chosen to join the MEK because she wanted freedom for the people; her husband turned her in and she was arrested. Every day they would announce her name on the loudspeaker that she had repented to break other women. They took me to her but I didn't recognize her she was so badly tortured. When she looked me in the eye I recognized her, she did not tell the interrogators who I was. When they realized they could not get any information, they executed her. I was in prison for more than five years, not even a day would suffice to tell you everything I saw. There is a book to be written — *The Price of Remaining a Human Being*. Another friend called it *Looking the Monster in the Eye*. Another female colleague wrote a book called *Leila's Smile*; another *Frontier of a Dream*; *The Islands of Suffering*. In these books you get sense of what happened in the regime.

"On February 8, 1982, the MEK SND command eighteen other members of the MEK were killed when the IRGC attacked a home. They took the bodies to Evin Prison, brought bodies to prison saying that the MEK is finished, to compel and break morale, so all would repent. They put the bodies all in a row in Evin Prison, taking prisoners from each cell and each ward to see the dead bodies, asking us to spit on the dead bodies. They took three series of prisoners from three different wards to see the bodies, but while expected them to lose morale, the exact opposite happened — they became a source of inspiration to all the prisoners, demonstrating to them the price you have to pay. When they took them, the prisoners would stand and salute to pay respect. They executed everyone who saluted, and stopped doing any more of this.

Speaker #4:

"During the presidential parliamentary elections, many MEK women were nominated, including Ashraf Rajavi, Talivani candidate from Tehran. Pro-regime thugs would attack gatherings and prevent us from speaking. One time they forced us to cancel an election campaign, when political activities were still allowed. Hezbollah thugs would hit, injure and kill activists.

Speaker #1:

"This level of resistance, by women, the sacrifices they have made in the prisons, necessitated women have a place in leadership of the MEK, especially since thirty percent of martyrs of MEK are by women. That is why, in 1985, Mrs. Rajavi, who had left in 1982 to go to Paris, having proven her qualifications as the most qualified woman, was chosen to be joint leader in June of 1985. When she became a joint leader the elevation and promotion of woman rose dramatically. Women attained leadership positions in all levels of the resistance, including the ILA. Commanding a battle is most serious. A woman has to have ability to make decisions, ability to command, and ability to persevere in the face of adversity, tremendous responsibility. It's arduous, and each and every woman had to overcome hesitance, and lack of self-confidence, to be leaders and commanders. Historically we did not believe in ourselves. Yes, we can be leaders; men did not believe as well. Given that we had to do this, despite whatever misgivings we had, with the help of one another, we succeeded in facing responsibilities. For each of us personally, it's not something we look forward to, when we looked at the responsibility, we could not say no, here we are now…thirty-three years…by learning from one another, we were able to gain qualifications to be on par with men in leadership of movement…woman tank commanders, military commanders, trained by Shah-captured instructors, passed on skills bought equipment from all over the world, learned maintenance, Huey helicopters, U.S. Army soldiers would see tanks and wished my soldiers took care of American Abrams tanks, like T-55s…maneuvers all the time, eternal light 3/88, a lot of Iranian commanders spoke of MEK women fighting; were exasperated about how MEK women fought before [they] all ran out of ammo and were killed by the regime.…women have to be on par with every part of this struggle.

"U.S. acted as an obstacle in taking away weapons, the MEK is ready to move forward.

"We are the voice for those who did not make it out of prison."

Witnesses to the 1988 Massacre

In 1988, the mullahs' regime, threatened by the mere existence of the MEK, decided to murder all MEK prisoners. The massacre was ghoulish, and the blood flowed. Many were hung over swimming pools, to collect the blood.

The testimony of these victims is delivered verbatim, word for word. I did not feel any literary right to change their revelations in any way, so please excuse any grammar or other literary errors.

The five men filed into the room and took their places around the table. There was an obvious sadness about all of them. Most of the members of the MEK I had talked to at Camp Ashraf were cheerful and full of life, even as they recounted their abuse by the Iranian regime.

These men were different.

They were survivors of the infamous 1988 massacre where the mullahs executed over thirty thousand members of the MEK, emptying the prisons in a short period of time — a few weeks, rivalling Hitler in their efficiency.

They took their seats at the table around me and waited to revisit their own private hell. The expressions on their faces made me realize the pain I was putting them through; however, the ordeal was necessary, in order to tell the world of the evil they had experienced firsthand.

***

Mahmoud Royaee was sixteen years old when he heard about the MEK. He became a sympathizer in 1980 after the revolution. He was arrested two years later at the age of eighteen, after being caught reading MEK publications. He was transferred to Evin Prison in Tehran.

#1 Mahmoud Royaee:

"I was a witness to interrogations and the extraction of confessions so traumatic that I have not even seen them in horror movies," he declared as his face exploded into lines of worry and stress remembering the events so long ago. "I won't give you all the details, but I experienced over two hundred forms of torture. I have written and documented them.

"I was summoned before a judge, a court, whatever you want to call it. There were no lawyers, no judge, no attorneys, just a mullah and the IRGC (Islamic Revolutionary Guard Corps agents). The judge read the charges; he didn't allow me to respond. He simply asked one question — 'Are you willing to take part in a television interview to repent?'

"I said no. The guard then violently dragged me out of the courtroom. After that, in a few days, I was transferred to Qezel Hesar Prison, where convicted (non-political) prisoners were being held. I thought, okay, I have been convicted, so I will serve my time with no abuse. It is just ten years in prison.

"I was wrong. During those ten years, I experienced a great deal of violence and psychological torment. I will only cite one example.

"As soon as I entered prison, my head was forcibly shaved. They also shaved my eyebrows, and forced me to eat them. They told me, 'Now you know the place you'll be spending time at.'

"The most shocking incident of all was the massacre of 1988. It was planned a year in advance, and implemented in August 1988. The regime murdered en masse virtually all of the prisoners without any reason or justification. These were people who had not been sentenced to death even by the regime's kangaroo courts. They were only supposed to spend some time in prison. There were one hundred people who had completed their prison terms in one ward. The regime hanged them as well, even the people who were sick and suffering from incurable diseases. They executed them all.

"There's a list of people who were paralyzed or sick with leprosy or other afflictions. They were all executed. This was inconceivable to many of the families. It was so shocking that when the regime told the parents their children were dead, some suffered heart attacks. The regime collected information about these families as well. In some cases, Khomeini's fatwa (religious decree) ordering the massacre went beyond just the execution of political prisoners. It included killing the families as well.

"When I completed my prison term, I decided to conduct research and collect documents and evidence so the outside world could find out about this massacre. It was then that I came to realize the real depths of the tragedy. I realized that the regime virtually destroyed a generation of Iranians in every city. It was a genocide. I published the results of my investigations in five volumes in 1997. I have put in writing the early years of the prison experience, and also the steps they took in secret to prepare for the massacre, and the massacre itself.

"In my investigations, I came to realize that we had no information about the prisoners. For instance, we have no information about prisoners in the northwest, western, or southwest Iran. The regime destroyed all the documents.

"I came across documents only recently that showed how the regime took some prisoners out of the facilities, and mutilated them with daggers or machetes. In the cities of Tabriz and Zanjan, they murdered them using brutal and horrific methods. In the southwest, they put prisoners in sacks and shot them. We don't even know everything that happened because not even a single prisoner survived in these areas. I my view, it was the greatest crime committed in contemporary world history after the end of World War II."

"I want to emphasize two points; this is a very small part of a major catastrophe. We haven't shared ninety percent of what we know. For example, we haven't told you about the MEK female members in the 1980s. What makes this case very unique is that they had a choice between living or dying. If they would not have said they were supporters of the MEK, they would not have been hanged. They chose not to do that. They were trying to get ahead of one another in order to sacrifice their lives. All had tremendous love for life and had developed deep bonds with others and their friends. But, their love of life and enthusiasm for freedom prompted them to obtain eternal life. We are still continuing investigations into the massacre. The important point is that those who ran the 1988 'death committees' are still occupying senior positions within the regime. One person responsible for the prisons was the regime's Minister of Justice for sixteen years. The Minister of Interior was an intelligence officer, as was the justice minister under Rouhani, who is now his senior advisor for judiciary affairs. Rouhani's presidential rival, mullah Ebrahim Raisi, was the prosecutor and was first deputy to the head of judiciary in Iran, then became in charge of the richest religious endowment. The regime has announced that he would be the next head of judiciary in Iran. What I want to emphasize is the people who were responsible were not prosecuted, or isolated, they now hold high-level positions in the regime. Now people who were not even born in 1988, despite all the regime's efforts to put a lid on this massacre, are seeking justice for the massacre and its victims."

***

Before the second survivor began sharing his ordeal, another survivor, Mohammed Zand, related his story to me, he had another brief story he wanted to tell, which he felt would impact his testimony and the project we were jointly attempting – to tell the story of the MEK.

#2 Mohammed Zand:

"Howard Baskerville was an American missionary in Iran and joined the constitutional revolutionaries fighting in East Azerbaijan Province, northwest Iran, in the early part of the twentieth century. He established a unit called the savior unit. The American ambassador at the time told him not to join the revolution because the United States was neutral in the fight between the monarch and the revolutionaries. But, he had two very famous sayings...

"The first was, 'Before being an American, I am a human being!' he told the ambassador.

"Secondly, he said, 'The difference between me and the Iranians is that I found my liberation in a different country. These people are fighting for their freedom in their country and it is my duty to help them. To defend this reality, you cannot hide behind any excuse.'

"He was killed in the revolution. The British ambassador said at the time his funeral was the most impactful funeral he had ever seen.

"When I saw you and heard about your decision to write this book, I had a sense, you are following the generation of Howard Baskerville. It is important that the truth be told. That is why, when you write the book, please tell this part of American history. We are proud of Baskerville. There is a statue of Howard Baskerville for his contribution in the Provincial capital, Tabriz.

"I was born into a religious family. My father worked for an American oil company in Tehran. He had helped to build some mosques. There was a Friday prayer leader in Tehran; my father would give him a dollar every time he came and spoke at our mosque, because we were Muslims. We were also human beings.

"When the mullahs came, they destroyed everything. But, before all else, they massacred humanity itself. For example, at

Camp Ashraf, when our protection was given to the Iraqi government, they installed 300 loudspeakers blasting propaganda against us around the clock — 24/7. This was exactly the same type of torture the regime used while I was in prison. In our cells and wards, we constantly heard sounds through the loud speakers. The noise was only cut off when there were executions, so we would be forced to hear them. The executions happened every night between three to five in the morning. The regime would kill them by firing squad. The only thing we heard, instead of the horrible abusive noise, was the sound of gunfire and coup de grace shots.

"I was arrested in 1981. They put me on a bench, tied up my hands and feet, and stretched me forward, and even tied up my big toe. The interrogator would demand, 'Tell us what you know!' I refused. They took me to the cleric to get judgment, and to torture, exactly like ISIS. In fact, the clerical regime in Iran is the grandfather of ISIS. They would take thick electric cables, with your arms extended forward, and legs extended the other way and lash the area beneath your stomach. As another form of torture, one person would sit on your back, pull your head up and stuff a dirty cloth in your mouth, and they would flog the soles of your feet. Blood would spew from the soles of your feet. They did it so many times. They would make you jump up and down on your feet to stop the swelling and bleeding.

"But this was not even the worst form of torture. The real torture was watching the person next to you being tortured, especially a mother or a child. You would hear the mother scream. They would flog the mother. Her four-year-old child would scream and cry. If you tried to console the baby, they would beat the child again, then again the tortured person. These scenes continued day, after day, after day in Evin Prison. The prisoners were sleep deprived, in solitary confinement. In the eyes of the regime's guards, we did not deserve to be alive.

"In February 1981, the prisoners protested because they had not received a cigarette ration. They were told, "You should have been killed already. If Khomeini issues the fatwa, we will bring a .50 caliber gun to prison and kill each and every one of you. This man was a plumber before he became a warden. We were told none of us would leave the prison alive.

"My trial was on September 27, 1981. My brother had already been executed. However, there was a huge demonstration in Tehran organized by the MEK, and my trial date was postponed. I was taken to an upper floor in the prison. I saw sitting on the bottom floor a huge number of protesters who had been arrested on the streets. We then saw the entire floor filled with MEK supporters who were chanting, 'Death to Khomeini!'

"They would bring a group of them to the third floor, every half hour, for a kangaroo trial. In the trial, they would take their names and a mullah asked them why they were arrested. Then they would take fifty to one hundred people and execute them. Several thousand had been arrested, but somehow I got mixed up in this group. Two days later, I heard two of the IRCG members talking to one another; they said 1,810 had been executed. Everyone arrested had been executed. The MEK estimated 1,400 but the IRCG put the death toll higher. Some of those arrested were wounded and had been taken to hospital. They were executed the night of the day they were brought back to prison. This mass murder was a sign of what was to come later.

"Of course, the regime was calling us 'terrorists.' I was given a life sentence. As I mentioned earlier, my brother was among the first to have been executed. We were sitting in the ward one day. Two days earlier, the regime had cut off our access to newspapers and TV. We staged a strike to protest. They picked a few of us staging the strike. They beat us, broke one of my ribs, and I was returned to my cell. When they called out the names, my brother's was among them. He gave me his ring. And, he never returned.

"When I went to my trial, the first thing they told me was that they had hanged my brother. I told them that I used to be an MEK sympathizer but now I wanted to live my personal life. I was put back into solitary confinement and they beat me three times a day, asking me to write what I knew about my friends. I tried to commit suicide but failed. I refused to write about my friends.

"The executions continued until August 6th. Then they began to execute non-MEK prisoners. The non-MEK members refused to cite the Islamic prayer. So, the regime executed them. This is what ISIS did later. So, ISIS took a page straight out of the mullahs' playbook.

"After the massacre was over in 1988, they brought those who had survived to one location. The first person I saw was Mahmoud. 160 survived. Out of several thousand prisoners, in twenty different wards, only 160 had remained.

"My father came and asked what had happened. I said I had no idea and asked him to try and find out. They called my father from Evin Prison and told him they had hanged his other son. He had asked, 'Why? He was only sentenced to ten years in prison.' In response, they threatened him. They told my father if you give us his birth certificate, we will tell you where to find his grave. He refused. So, they held my father for three days, carried out a mock execution against him several times, but he still refused to cooperate with them. So, they let him go but warned him against holding a funeral for his son. My father responded that he would organize the biggest funeral possible for his son, and that is exactly what he did.

"One of my brother's friends was engaged. Even in the year 2000, his fiancé was still in mourning and wearing black. She has not married to this day.

"Another person was an international badminton star. His father, upon hearing that he had been hanged, had a heart attack and died. This was the case for many families. Thirty thousand were massacred by 1988. There is a total of 120,000 victims during the regime's reign. The executions that occurred between 1981 to 1988 went on continuously, non-stop. The regime used the pretext of the war with Iraq (Fifth Column) to execute political prisoners. Because my father was friends with some clerics, my sentence was reduced. He contacted an ayatollah and I received a reduced sentence from life to twelve years. That is why they did not execute me. I then joined the MEK in 2000 and I'm very proud to share my story.

"Tell our story to the rest of the world. There are others who would also be happy to provide information so the world discovers these tragedies."

***

#3 Hussein Farsi:

"I was a supporter of the MEK during the 1979 revolution. I was sixteen at the time and I was arrested when I was 18 years old. Today, we've talked about how the trials were carried out in prisons. I was tortured after my arrest. They struck my head so many times that it was broken in multiple places. I had bandages all over my head and face. They blindfolded me and I could not see anything. They took the detainees into the 'court room'. There was a guy sitting there asking questions. He wrote six questions. I provided a written response to the six questions. I was asked to sign the sheet and leave. They put my blindfold back on and I left. I then found out that that was my trial. It took 15 minutes. I was sentenced to three years in prison.

"At the end of my prison term, they said I had been issued a sentence to repent. I asked what it meant and they said I have to stay in prison until I actually repent. There were no laws for this. Khomeini had ordered that no one should be released until they repent (from supporting the MEK). Those who were given this sentence were essentially in legal limbo. I was released after spending an additional year in prison. But I was arrested again two years after my release. They claimed that I had called friends outside of Iran who were sympathetic to the MEK. I had a second trial. This time, a mullah was sitting in the room; he was the pros-ecutor, judge, and jury for the court. The trial lasted ten minutes. He asked me to sign what he had written. And that was my trial.

"In July 1984, a cleric named Majid Ansari, who came to visit us as the representative of Ayatollah Hossein-Ali Montazeri, at the time, Khomeini's designated successor. He is now dubbed one of the most prominent reformers. Once he came to visit Qezel He-sar Prison, and asked why we didn't have lawyers during our trial and no defense. "You have the right to access a lawyer," he said. But there was one small problem. The problem was that if a law-yer would dare to defend a political prisoner in these 'trials,' he would be executed the same day. Even now, when you see law-yers at the so-called revolutionary courts, they are not really de-fending their clients.

"[The current regime supreme leader] Ali Khamenei has a brother named Hadi. In the 1980s, Hadi Khamenei was an inter-rogator and torturer. They mutilated political prisoners in Evin. In 1982, Khomeini sent Hadi Khamenei to visit prisons. He had been sent to investigate if human rights were being violated, and to look for signs of torture. This is while he himself was a torturer!

"The regime's courts gave legal justification to torture. In 1985, when I was being interrogated, my judge would issue religious verdicts for torture. They would take us to a room with blindfolds on. The regime's agent would say the prisoner is not talking. Then Hadi Khamenei would order a very rare form of punishment, called chicken roast, [which meant] tying up the prisoners and lashing them with cables.

"In 1987, I was sent to Karaj. Upon our arrival in the prison yard, they had set up what they called a 'tunnel.' There were two parallel rows of IRCG agents standing with batons and knives. When the prisoner started walking in between the two rows, the agents would beat them from both sides. Then we went to the third floor. There were two hundred prisoners on this floor. It was winter time and cold. They ordered us to undress. The guards moved in to beat us with cables and sticks; they beat us for a full hour. I had been on a hunger strike for three days. I couldn't even walk. Their treatment was brutal and pure savagery. When we asked what we were charged with, they wanted us to say we were sympathizers of 'hypocrites' (the regime's derogatory term to refer to the MEK).

"If we said we were sympathizers, we would be beaten again quite badly. We could not say 'Mujahedin-e Khalq' as the term was banned. This was critical and decisive for the 1988 massacre.

"In August 1988, they took myself and others in front of a judge. We had no idea this was a trial. We all had blindfolds on. They called it a 'clemency court,' and it was empowered to issue amnesty for prisoners. Among them was the prosecutor general, Morteza Eshraghi. Sitting at the table in the middle was mullah Hossein-Ali Nayyeri, the religious judge, and to his left a younger cleric, whom I later found out was Mostafa Pourmohammadi. The judge would ask us questions as we were made to stand in front of him. He asked each individual's name, age, and what we were charged with. If you said you were a sympathizer of the MEK, the trial would end, and a verdict would immediately be written. All three of the people I mentioned would sign it. The whole thing

lasted no more than two or three minutes. If you avoided saying
that you are a sympathizer of the MEK, they would ask additional
questions. Among other questions, they would ask: 'Are you willing to condemn the MEK?'

"At that time, I was being held at Gohardasht Prison in Karaj. I
was a witness to the massacre, for four or five days morning and
night. I was in the corridor of the prison leading up to the courtroom. One time late at night, one of the prison guards asked the
warden if he could call his wife, as she had become sick and was
taken to the hospital. That's when we found out that all the
phones and communications in and out of the prison had been cut
off. Only one telephone line was available, to which the religious
judge had access. We found out later that even prison guards were
not allowed to leave the premises, spending the entire time in the
prison as the massacre was going on. The bitter irony was that the
warden, Mohammad Moqiseh, was also acting the supervising
prosecutor of the court, which meant that he had both an execu-
tive and a judicial position at the same time. So, he essentially he
was his own supervisor and overseer. Currently, he is head of the
28th branch of the revolutionary court in Tehran. He was very active in the massacre. This is how they massacred everyone.

"I want you to know this story had two sides. On one side,
there was savagery, barbarism, and absolute inhumanity. On the
other side, however, there were also stories of perseverance, resistance, defiance and humanity created by the prisoners. Those
who were killed were the most educated, enlightened children of
Iran.

[Farsi breaks down at this point, weeping uncontrollably.]

"It is true that the mass murderers were savage and brutal, but on the other side, you saw the height of valiant and admirable defiance and resistance against dictatorship. *[Weeping uncontrollably]* Although my own brother was killed and as savage as Khomeini was, these heroes and heroines, resisted against his savagery with one word - MEK. They gave their lives for an ideal, for which the MEK was fighting.

"In one particular instance, a forty-seven-year-old musician was taken to this so-called court. They threatened him, told him to leave, and he was hanged. Thirty of us were in one cell. Seven survived. In other cells, there were 110 prisoners and five or six survived. The reality is that when we were asked a question, we said we had been a sympathizer and now just wanted to go on with our normal lives. In a sense, we didn't take a stance, otherwise, we wouldn't be here today. I didn't stand up for the MEK. They killed anyone who did so. It was an ideological issue; they had to kill the ideal.

"Then they started murdering the Marxists. They asked are you Marxist or Muslim. They asked about your father. If the father was Muslim, the verdict would be death. If the person said he/she was a Marxist, they would say pray three times a day, receive ten lashes, and convert to Islam. It was shocking for us.

"Evin Prison was nearly empty after the massacre. Prior to it, the prison had been overflowing with prisoners, but no longer. I still didn't know about the real scope and scale of the massacre. We didn't know what was happening. We began to find out about the real scope gradually. When I left Iran, I was still researching and investigating this massacre and searching for more details. We are in contact with the families in Iran. They send us information. A friend went to a cemetery in Iran; he sent me pictures of a mass grave. We came across a name that had not been on our list. We thought he had been released. We realized that a few weeks before he had been hanged. Another friend was released. His wife was a pharmacist. He and his wife were killed in 1988 when they tried to leave Iran. Just the other night we came across a case with the name of a victim we did not have on our list. There was another case last year. A young man contacted us through the internet. He said I did not know my father was a political activist. He was a year old at the time of his father's death. He was told that his father died of natural causes. Then his grandfather told him his father had been with the MEK and had been hanged in 1988. His grandfather had hidden this fact from him for thirty years and he contacted us because he wanted to know what had happened.

"I am telling you all this to convey the extent of this massacre. After thirty years, there is a lot that remains unknown about the massacre of 1988.

"I hope and I pray that once we overthrow this regime we can open the files and find out how many were killed and where they are buried. What you are doing is truly invaluable as the world has tried to cover up this heinous crime against humanity for the past thirty years. In 1990, even the United Nations referred to it only in passing and did nothing. So, what you are trying to do is commendable. This book will be there for all the people of the world to judge for themselves.

"Thank you."

***

Asghar Mehdizadeh is a tall thin man. He is also a broken man. You can see it in his face as he talks. He is a man who has faced more than any other human being should have to. The emotional scars are palpable. He is physically frail. He began to speak quietly and the room is as quiet as a morgue.

#4 Asghar Mehdizadeh:

"I was born in northern Iran, Gilan Province, near the Caspian Sea. This is where the legendary freedom fighter, Mirza Kuchek Khan, had his headquarters. My father was a farmer and poor. Many of my friends went to university. I dreamt of becoming a doctor, but that coincided with the revolution in 1979, so I decided not to pursue my studies. In 1979, we were blessed with a revolution because of the sacrifices made by the MEK years before. A friend of mine, who was studying computer science, was arrested. I became a political activist because of him.

"Another friend, who had a bachelor's degree in theology, spent two years at Evin Prison during the Shah's dictatorship. In early 1979, he led anti-Shah demonstrations in our city and played an important role in organizing demonstrations. We had four or five martyrs in our small city already, but despite all of this sacrifice, Khomeini stole the leadership of the revolution. The people elected my friend as mayor of our town. The MEK had many sup-porters in our city, such that when we held the first parliamentary elections in 1980, their candidate received the most votes. But after declaring a run-off, they eliminated him in the second round. Then Massoud Rajavi visited the province and he was greeted by over 300,000 people who listened to his speech. One of our politi-cal demands was that our people deserve at the very least the min-imum standards of freedoms. We had an association in our city but the IRCG suppressed it. They occupied our association. We went to take it back, almost a thousand of us. They were opposed to us engaging in such activity and we confronted them for sev-eral hours. The IRCG arrested twenty of us. I was taken to prison at Rasht city. I spent four months in prison, where I was tortured and beaten.

"A local guard commander made us go through mock execu-tions on a couple of occasions. Ultimately, we were released but we could see the political environment was becoming more and more suppressed.

"On June 20, 1981, the reign of terror started; they killed anyone who opposed the regime. We couldn't walk around in public. One time, seven or eight of us went to help the local rice farmers. The IRCG surrounded us. The farmer told us about it and we tried to escape. One of our friends, who used to be a soccer player, was shot and killed. The rest of us managed to escape the IRGC's siege. When they killed him, the family demanded his body. The IRCG told the family they must first pay 10,000 riyals (or 120 dollars based on the exchange rate at the time) for each bullet.

"The IRCG would not allow the family to bury their child or to have a funeral. My friend, who was the mayor of our city, had his house set on fire. They also confiscated his car and arrested him in 1981. They told him that he had spoken in favor of the MEK. He asked to speak to family at least once, but they refused and executed him. His wife and child came for a visit to the prison and had a box of sweets. But, the regime informed them that he had been executed. In response, thousands of people poured into the streets in protest and there were clashes between the people and the regime's forces. The regime took the body and buried him in an unknown location. He was the most prominent figure in our city. The member of parliament from our city was murdered, too, in order to intimidate and terrorize our tortured city. They left his dead body dangling from a pole to instill fear among the population.

"I went to Tehran and was arrested in early 1982 and taken to Evin Prison. A couple more people were arrested. When we entered the ward, they asked what are you charged with. Whomever said supporting the MEK, they would take him immediately to the torture chamber. They beat us for so long in order to try and extract any information. They beat us to the point that we were close to death. During my imprisonment, I saw the deaths of several of my friends as a result of such beatings. One of my friends was severely tortured but remained defiant. He claimed that he would take the regime's agents to other MEK members, but he was lying to them. He said he would take them to a rendezvous point outside prison and he fooled them. They took him to the torture room and that is the last time I saw him. When I asked

about his whereabouts, nobody knew what had happened to him.
It was savage and barbaric torture. They would flog the soles of
our feet so much that they would swell up and become double the
normal size of an average foot. After a few days, we were transferred to the general ward — a 2 by 6 meter room, with forty to
sixty prisoners inside.

"During one night in Ramadan, they took several MEK members, including two from our cell, to be tortured. They used cables,
iron rods, and wooden sticks to beat them all over their bodies.
When they brought them back to their cells in the morning hours,
their heads, necks, and arms, were all bruised and fractured.

"In our ward, there were Iranians from all walks of life. There
were engineers, students, and one was a doctor. After a year of
interrogations, they told the doctor that he must collaborate. He
refused, so they executed him.

"Another gentleman had been studying for a master's degree
in architecture. They arrested and tortured him continuously for
twenty-four hours. They flogged him so much that his kidneys
stopped functioning and he had to go on dialysis to survive. There
was an engineer who spent six months in solitary confinement.
He was under so much psychological pressure that all his hair
turned grey. His father couldn't recognize him. He actually had
to assure his father by telling him, 'I'm your son.' They all were
executed.

"When we were in our cells at night, we could hear gunfire and
coup de grace shots against prisoners. They relocated me. They
would force us every night to go to a prayer area in the prison.

Whenever Khomeini wanted a large number of executions, he would summon the IRCG to his office. People were calling Khomeini 'bloodsucker'. In February 1982, I heard Khomeini had issued a fatwa (religious decree) to kill several thousand people. They took two to three people from our cell. At Evin, they transferred me to solitary confinement for several months. While there, I could hear the cries of female prisoners one floor below. Of course I couldn't sleep. Then I went to my 'trial' at a 'court', which was located below my solitary cell. The judge was the same individual that Farsi spoke about earlier. The trial lasted only two minutes. He said anyone who still maintains his stance about supporting the MEK will be executed, period. He continued: If you agree to do an interview and make confessions, we will give you a prison term instead. If not, you will be hanged. If we come to the conclusion that you have truly repented, you will be released.

"I witnessed the trials of some of my friends. After the execution of thirty of my friends, in the middle of 1983, I was sentenced to seventeen years in prison. Until 1985, most prisoners were in solitary. In 1985, they changed the prison warden, a mullah. He claimed that his methods will be different and added: I will provide you with some amenities and privileges if you do what I tell you to do.

"He said: 'I'm going to do something to break your resistance.' He brought a few people who had repented, and forced everyone to engage in collective prayer sessions. But after confronting people who remained defiant, he told us: 'You are all hypocrites, none of you has recanted' In 1986, he said: 'We're not going to deal with you until I have some more time, then we will decide your fate.'

"He prevented us from exercising if we did so in groups. We were in solitary, a 4x8 meter room with no windows. After a couple of hours there, it felt like I was suffocating. If you banged on the door in protest, they would open the door and beat you. In early 1988, after our collective exercise session, armed prison guards came to our ward. They said: If Khomeini issues the order, we will shoot all of you. One time I complained about the lack of facilities, and they relocated us. The guard told me: Whoever says they are a sympathizer of the MEK, they must pay the price for their convictions.

"In 1987, they classified the prisoners based on the type of sentence they had received. We were under intense pressure. In 1988, they first tortured everybody. There was a group that had come from Mashhad. They would summon them and asked what are you charged with. They beat them with iron rods. We would all continue to say we are MEK supporters.

"On August 24, 1988, they had given all of us time to walk in the prison yard. All of us had blindfolds on when we returned to our cells. They took us out, and put us in front of an assistant prosecutor. He pretended to be very polite. He was trying to give the impression that conditions had changed, so it was no problem to claim that one is supportive of the MEK. The next day in the afternoon, they cut everyone's access to television. On Friday morning, an armed guard with a walkie-talkie in his hand came and browsed the yard. Saturday was supposed to be a day for family visits. We got ready to see our families. We also were supposed to be allowed to go shopping at the prison store. But there were no family visits, and no shopping allowed.

"Around ten in the morning, they took away twelve prisoners. I never saw them again. At 12:30, I was looking outside from a small window. I saw a guard taking away five blindfolded prisoners in the yard. They went to the washroom. Those in blindfold were made to stand facing the wall. He punched the wall. I still remember that scene. Then he took them out of the big red gate. There was a short alleyway and a warehouse that had a small red door. They took everyone inside the warehouse. After thirty minutes, the IRCG came out to the open-air area. There were two individual guards, wearing t-shirts. They were sweating because once they took them into the warehouse, one of the prisoners had confronted them and they had hanged them all. They executed twenty people on that Saturday.

"After breakfast the next day, we looked out the window; we realized what we had seen. He told us to take our belongings and come out of the cell. They set up a gauntlet. The took us to the cell opposite the one we were in. I had to go back and forth several times. The guard asked another person, "What are you charged with?", and he shouted "supporting the honorable MEK." Immediately they took him away to execute him. They began to clean the cell. After about half an hour, the security guard came and told all of us to go to the large mess hall. He asked about the charges against us and what sentence we have received. He took 13 of us in blindfold to the prosecutor. He gave them a form to fill out. That night, they took us back to solitary. The next day, they took us out of solitary to the main corridor. The security guard was there. He would ask us how many years we are in for, and what our charges are, and make us sit outside where the prosecutor was. Then they took us into the room where the 'trials' were being held.

"We were there from the morning on Monday to about 8 o'clock in the evening. Then they took the prisoners back in groups of 10, 15, or 20 until the following Monday. When they asked me what is the charge, I said I'm a 'hypocrite;' he hit me in the head. He said, "Damn you, why are you saying this?" He gave me a form; I read it and tore it apart. Then they put me back in solitary. The following Monday they asked the same questions. Then they handed me over to two IRCG guards, who took me to the previous location where I was in prison. As soon as I entered, I noticed the rotten food that was there. I realized the last prisoner in the cell had been taken to be executed on the day that the food was brought. There were bags and belongings of other prisoners. There were also farewell notes on each one of the bags. "We are going to be hanged," the notes said. "Send Massoud Rajavi our greetings."

"When we went to take a shower, we heard cries of women from the floor below. I wanted to inform them that everyone had been hanged, but the guards came in, threw me into the bathroom and beat me. I was unconscious. I gained consciousness at around 10:00 p.m. I looked at the solitary cells; the lights were on in some of them. When I turned on the light in my cell, a guy inside realized I was there. I noticed he was one of my friends. He told me they took everyone into the mess hall. He said they took me there and wanted me to collaborate with them. Four to five of his relatives had already been executed. His family met him for the last time. They said we have already lost five relatives, so do something so that they won't hang you. He said he told his family I would love to live, I don't want to die, I'll try to do as much as I can to stay alive, but I cannot abandon my principles and ideals. He said he would never live in humiliation and he reminded them of the betrayal of the Tudeh Party. So why do you want me to be called someone who had betrayed his fellow compatriots? They ultimately hanged him.

"The next morning the guard came looking for me; I put on some clothes and he took me to the mess hall where they were hanging people. I peeked from underneath the blindfold. When I got to the cleric, I saw the area was full of prisoners. I sat down in a corner and asked what was going on. "Are you new here?" the prisoners asked. They told me the regime takes a group to be hanged every hour. A guard came and said, "Those who want to go to heaven and drink milk and honey, follow me" (in other words, the people that are steadfastly supportive of the MEK). 12 people got up to go. Many others got up in a rush to join the 12. The other IRCG guard asked, "Why are you trying to get ahead of everyone?" The prisoner shouted, 'Do you want to know why?' The guard said, 'Yes.' The prisoner told the guard, 'Unless you are one of us, you can never understand. You will never be in our shoes and in our place.' He took a group of them inside. After a half hour, the guard came and took me inside the mess hall and removed my blindfold. I saw a heap of bodies, executed prisoners, one on top of another.

"The mess hall was 60 by 30 meters; it had a stage, from which twelve ropes hung and underneath each rope there was a chair.

The people that they brought in would literally and voluntarily try to jump on the chair themselves. Their morale and passion were exemplary. They would shout, 'Hail to the MEK! Hail to Massoud Rajavi!' They would also make reference to the third Shiite Imam, Hussein.[1]"

At this point, the translator breaks down and cries at length...

"The IRCG members were in shock and in awe of such courage and raw bravery. When I saw these prisoners showing so much valor, I felt pity for myself for not defending the MEK with the same degree of passion. I never thought they would hang everybody but I realized the regime was hell-bent on hanging all of them. At that time, they brought another 12 under the noose, and they, too, climbed on the chair. Again, the prisoners repeated chants along the lines that victory will be ours, we will soon triumph, long live the MEK's National Liberation Army. The judge then realized these scenes of courage were having a big impact even on the guards themselves. He saw the resolve and the determination of MEK supporters. I could hear the cleric saying, 'Yes, they are hanging them, but with such bravery, such a mark of defiance.'

"So the judge came up and started kicking the first three chairs away; I saw the remaining nine prisoners kicking away their own chairs that were underneath them. I lost my mental balance and

---

[1]Hussein bin Ali, the son of the first Shiite Imam Ali and grandson of Prophet Mohammad, is a revered Islamic figure. He died in the battle of Karbala while fighting oppression and injustices of his time.

passed out. I woke up noticing the guard was pouring water on my face. I gained consciousness and they were back dragging bodies by their feet to the door, loading them onto trucks and the trucks drove away.

"If the executed people had any personal belongings, the regime would steal it. Of course the prisoners knew this so they would destroy anything that was worth something, so the guards wouldn't take them.

"They took me to my previous cell. I had lost my psychological balance. They took me to a cell where I saw Mahmoud and Hossein. We had all witnessed incredible bravery and were in awe. Outside the prisons, the families were defiant and resistant as well. I had my first family visit in December of that year. First I saw my mother and asked her how my friends at Evin Prison were. She told me they were all dead. I asked about others. They were all dead. For me, after the massacre, every day lasts like 1,000 days; Before the massacre, all the years in prison seemed like nothing to me. At any rate, I was released in 1994.

"All of the families who knew I was alive would invite me to their homes after my release. I went to meet the families of some of the martyrs; they saw me and hugged me and said you smell of our son. I felt very ashamed of what they said to me. I went to the family of another victim; her mother was blind. She asked me when is my son coming home and I didn't know what to tell her. One time I went to the home of the wife and children of one of the people who had been hanged. He was a language teacher and had been hanged in Rasht. I spoke with his wife; she told me the regime authorities had told them he had not been hanged, but was sent to Lebanon on a mission. I told them that they hanged everybody and that they should not trust the regime. She had a five-year-old daughter named Matin. The daughter turned to the mother and said Mom, this uncle (me) is telling us that my dad has been hanged.

"I had heard they buried all the victims in mass graves; I tried to go and see these mass graves. They told me if go there they will arrest you and imprison you again. I saw them all executed, so why should I be afraid of being arrested? I saw a piece of land with about 6 by 7 meters of cement poured on it. I said some prayers and came back. Later on I heard from my friends and others that prisoners in Rasht had been hanged naked. While they were digging mass graves, people had identified the driver of a bulldozer. So, they kept pointing him out as a traitor wherever he went. Many of the mothers would go to the graves and say prayers for the victims, but the regime authorities would arrest and harass them. There are many mass graves in northern Iran. They were shallow and limbs had surfaced out of the dirt and people realized they are graves. These happened in my own hometown, as well as other nearby towns.

"After I was released, someone told me that the family of one of the victims wants to know where I was. They lived in a city north of Tehran. I went to see them. The mother hugged and kissed me. When we sat down, she said my husband and I have searched everywhere and we have not found anything about the fate of our son. The father had only heard that his son had been hanged. The mother showed me two pictures. When I saw the son I realized he had been with us in our cell, but the name we had was different from what the mother told me. We realized for seven years that he had not divulged his real name to the regime's torturers. As a result, he had no family visits, nothing. He and several others like him had a lot of affection for Massoud Rajavi. All of them were hanged because of that. Nobody knows where they are; nobody knew their names.

"There were many similar cases. Some were released and captured again later. There are tons of similar examples.

"I myself spent three years in solitary confinement. There is a huge MEK presence in northern Iran.

"I want to say Massoud Rajavi helped me to summon the courage to talk about what I witnessed."

***

#5 *Assadollah Nabavi:*

"I was born in the town of Shahmirzad, on the outskirts of the city of Semnan, northeast of the capital. I spent thirteen years in prison. I was sixteen when I was arrested in 1985. I was involved in a campaign that called for freedom and peace and an end to the Iran-Iraq War. I always knew that the regime tortured people and that I would be tortured if arrested. But I could not imagine it the way it actually unfolded. I must say that our family was very supportive of the MEK. In early 1981, several of my cousins were ex-

ecuted and thirty members of my family were imprisoned. Therefore, I was not unfamiliar with the conditions in the prisons. I experienced torture. I was flogged. I tried to count the number of
lashes but I could never count more than one hundred, as I would
lose consciousness every time. After flogging us, they put us on a
trolley and moved us to the cell. This continued day after day.

"The prison had initially been a stable where they held horses
four hundred years ago. The walls were 80 centimeters thick. The
cries could never be heard.

"In 1988, I was sentenced to four years in prison. In the autumn
of 1987, there were twenty-five of us being held in a cell. They
called us out to send us to solitary confinement. They presented
us with papers and gave us half a day to respond to the questions
written on those papers. There were one hundred questions. The
questions were reminiscent of the era of Inquisition. They were
designed to glean from us where we stood politically. We replied
to the questions. We had no clue as to why we were asked to do
this.

"The massacre began in 1988. They were classifying and cate-
gorizing prisoners to determine what to do with them. They took
the first group, and the next day the next group, and so on.
Through our contacts, we realized they had taken a lot of the prisoners from other parts of the prison in order to execute them. Two
days before the massacre, on July 30th, we were cut off from family visits and TV. They gave furloughs to all the soldiers and
guards. Only veteran members of the IRGC remained. We realized this was an unusual and strange situation. They took me to

solitary. While there, I was able to communicate with another prisoner. He had been taken to trial and returned. He said we must write our last will. When he went to trial, the judge and a cleric associated with the Ministry of Intelligence had asked strange questions. He predicted that they were going to hang us. But I did not believe him.

"Three days later, they brought a woman who was severely tortured and laying on a trolley. We asked her about what's happening and where the others were. She said they are going to hang me. We were talking to her at night, and the very next morning they took her to be hanged. In less than three weeks, everyone at the prison was hanged. Only three survived. For those of us who survived, it was extremely difficult because we kept thinking about all of those who had been executed. They hanged two brothers in front of a fifteen-year-old friend. When they brought him out, he was still brave and in high spirits. They hanged him, too. There was a teacher who was married and had a child. His prison sentence was nearly complete but they executed him as well.

"I had a friend who was a university student. He had already completed his prison sentence. He was amongst the first to be hanged. I remember all their names. I keep repeating their names because it rekindles a love and affection I had for each and every one of them. I was kept in solitary for eighteen months. They were starving me. When I saw myself in the mirror, I didn't recognize myself because I had lost so much weight. When I was transferred at the end of 1989, other people who saw me couldn't believe it.

As a means of clemency, I was sentenced to fifteen years and released in 1998.

"When I got out, I had two impressions. One was, given the
scale of the massacre, the population should be completely demoralized. But on the contrary, I saw that the people in society
were very hopeful. I was surprised to see that the attraction to the
MEK had increased even more, in such a way that people wanted
to join their ranks. I know at least sixteen people who came to
Ashraf in Iraq. Secondly, I thought now that the massacre had finished, perhaps the families know about it. But, the authorities had
not informed the families and they had no clue at the time. Many
did not even know where the graves were, or that their relatives
had been hanged. Some were suspicious and made phone calls to
speak to their children in prison. They told one family simply that
their child was in Iran. They were trying to put pressure on and
psychologically torture the family. Even four years after, mothers
would still frequent the prison and they didn't know that their
child had been hanged. Every Monday, one of them would bring
a basket of fruit. The guards used to mock her. On her return, she
would give the fruit to the poor instead. The mother of one
woman who was executed had a funeral for her daughter. The
Ministry of Intelligence kidnapped the mother from the funeral.
She never returned home. Another friend who was released established contacts with the families of those executed. We worked
together in 2004 and 2005, and compiled a publication. Not many
were openly supportive but we could sense their sympathies. We
published five issues. The circulation was substantial. One day,
the Ministry of Intelligence raided our office and arrested both of

us. In 2006, I ended up in prison again. We placed a substantial bail, and they released us. We immediately left Iran, but my friend was again arrested at the cemetery of the 1988 massacre victims. He was hanged.

"When released from prison, I tried to go and visit families of some of the victims. What was surprising for me was that when I went to the villages in northern Iran, I saw the graves of the executed children in some people's backyards. Their parents had buried their beloved children in their own gardens. These graves had turned into public places of worship in the villages. Although I knew there had been a massacre, I was surprised to find out about the scale. It had left victims in virtually every city and village across Iran."

Camp Ashraf Falls

A conversation with survivors of Ashraf in Iraq

Speaker #1:

"[In] 2003, before the U.S. invasion of Iraq, the MEK announced impartiality. We received a message to stay in the camps and you will not be targeted. Unfortunately, we were targeted as part of a deal with the mullahs by the Americans, over fifty were killed. Most of our camps were destroyed. After that, we concentrated in Camp Ashraf. The first contact was with US SOF North Iraq, and we started discussions with the SOF CC, based on a cease fire agreement, LTC Tovo.

"General Odierno told us we would have to give up our weapons. He said was here to secure our surrender, with status of POWs under the Geneva Convention. Intimidation and a show of force were used, but when he came and met face to face, he was surprised at women negotiators. He had been briefed by the State Department and they did not tell the truth. It was an intelligence failure. State knew the Iraq invasion was engineered by Ahmed Chalabi, dragging the U.S. into the war. It was a major counterintelligence coup by Iran, the alleged hiding of Iraqi WMD. Later it was acknowledged that Chalabi was a double agent for Iran. He told the Americans we were hiding chemical weapons in Ashraf. We have a firetruck that is used to sanitize the chemical weapons at Ashraf. U.S. MPs came to the camp to take the fire truck, to check for chemical weapons. When Chalabi died, an Iranian web-site said the architect of the Iraqi invasion has died. *The treachery by Iran to get the U.S. to launch an invasion against their mortal enemy in Iraq is an untold story of the war.* The goal also was to get the MEK on the terrorist list. It was an agenda of the regime, playing with the U.S. Government. When he heard we are only out to bring down the regime in Iran, after two days of negotiations, the General was a sincere person. After negotiations ended, he stood in front of cameras and said MEK freedom fighters wanted democ-racy in Iran, and the U.S. should review a new designation as free-dom fighters.

"The MEK marked up the surrender document; we would not surrender. After nine hours of talks, negotiations, which were very honest, we reached the freedom fighter decision. This is not surrender. We had a collection of weapons in one place. We told the General we have been fighting for freedom since teenagers to fight against surrender, if you want to kill us go ahead, but we will not surrender. We then served him some Iranian and Italian food, and we were still on the terrorist list, laughing that he shouldn't negotiate with terrorists. After two days of negotiations, he advised to change the designation. Iranian demonization of the MEK is long and large; there is a singular focus on the MEK. They pushed the U.S. to bomb the camps. Many American commanders told us we are not terrorists. They had a one-year rotation think-ing they would be protecting terrorist organizations, but then they would leave as friends, a six-year mission.

"The MEK was to provide some understanding of the Iranian regime in Iraq; the Americans were ignorant of the IRGC. We told

DIA officers about the Quds Force, responsible for IEDs in Iraq. Of course there was difficulty to convince the MEK rank and file to hand over our weapons to the U.S. military. On May 17, Cent-Com issued a statement stating the MEK weapons were surrendered.

"General Odierno recognized the people who they were meeting — the MEK — had an ideal, and were extremely committed to that ideal. They were one of the most educated armies of the world, an all-volunteer army. While leadership agreed to hand over weapons, how do we convince rank and file to hand over the weapons, organizationally speaking? This was the most difficult task; they would write notes on equipment to say goodbye. It was very difficult. Junior U.S. officers were overtaken by emotion seeing the handover of weapons. MEK leadership said we were not allowed to fire at the U.S....while being bombed. When we met Odierno, we said we have two red lines — we will not surrender, you can capture. Two, our enemy is only the regime in Tehran, not the United States.

"Odierno's final agreement allowed the MEK to remain in uniform.

"The MEK told the U.S. and UK where they were, and they used information to bomb us. Then after the agreement, the U.S. took over protection of Camp Ashraf. We had to screen every individual at Ashraf privately, in the presence of U.S. officers, seven different agencies of the U.S. The U.S. took responsibility for protection, issued everyone a protected persons card, under 4th Geneva convention.

Massoud Rajavi – head of MEK in the early 1990s

Massound and Maryam Rajavi
MEK National Liberation Army in early 1990s Iraq

Massound Rajavi – National Liberation Army in the early 1990s Iraq

Maryam Rajavi – Free Iran Rally 2018

Massound and Maryam Rajavi
MEK National Liberation Army in early 1990s Iraq

MEK Camp Ashraf, Iraq 2012

Gates of MEK Camp Ashraf, Iraq, 2012

MEK National Liberation Army, Iraq, 1988

town of Manëz close to capital Tirana

MEK Camp Ashraf 3, Albania, 2018

MEK Camp Ashraf, Albania, 2022

MEK/PMOI Rally, Paris, 2023

L Todd Wood meeting with MEK member
Camp Ashraf 3, Albania, 2018

Kitchens prepare daily food for different tastes

L Todd Wood meeting with kitchen workers
Camp Ashraf 3, Albania, 2018

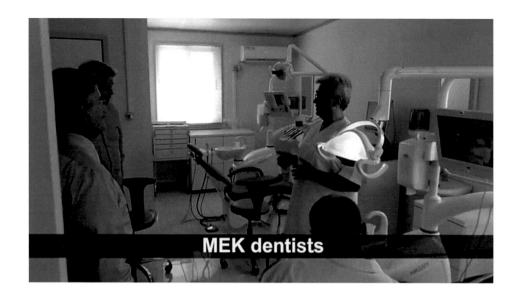

L Todd Wood meeting the MEK dentists
Camp Ashraf 3, Albania, 2018

L Todd Wood meeting with internet activist
Camp Ashraf 3, Albania, 2018

"10/05 - William Brandenberg retired, Dep CC Iraqi multinational forces.

"9/09. The U.S. handed over protection to Iraqi forces. The International Committee of the Red Cross opposed the documents for the turn over. The Iraqis were openly hostile and under the direction of Iran. Before this happened, we had good relations with the people of Iraq. The MEK was a buffer to Iranian interference in Iraq On the first day of Iraqi control, they laid siege — nobody could exit or enter. This was a new phase. The U.S. said laws of war no longer applied; however, the U.S. simply wanted to hand over this protection as Obama was negotiating with Iran. Obama wanted out for Iran. The agreement they signed with each member said until your final disposition in Iraq; in fact, the Geneva Convention is clear — if you hand over protection of a group of people, and their rights are not protected, the transferring party must take back protection. The U.S. wanted to wash its hands of the MEK. The Rand report came out — all our members wrote to the U.S. that we do not agree with the transfer. The U.S. military engaged another round of interviews with people, everyone said no to hand over protection to the Iraqis. The U.S. did the transfer despite their initial agreement to hand over. The Iraqis shutdown the gates, people could no longer come in and work. Medical treatment was almost impossible. No families were allowed to come to the camp. Ashraf became a large prison for all of us. When protection was handed over, the protection should have been handed over to the minister of interior of Iraq. "Maliki set up a committee formed by Iranian elements in Iraq, to handle Ashraf. The court in Spain issued a warrant for crimes against humanity.

"The Americans made a major miscalculation — that the Iraqi government was like a normal government and remained committed to its obligations. But of course we did not violate any laws. There were trilateral meetings for many months to reach an understanding. Iraq insisted we have to have their police inside Ashraf, meant to suppress and harass the residents. One, set up police. Two, move to another location. Three, eliminate everybody. The Americans were so naive, to think it was just a police station. We were involved with negotiations with the Iraqis; they said police must come inside the camp. They said why don't we meet after lunch? At some time the committee to suppress Ashraf had come to the camp and the meeting ended. We were supposed to meet after lunch. After lunch, Iraqi police attacked the camp and thirteen were killed, one thousand wounded, thirty-six captured. We started a hunger strike.

"Iraq issued statement we must leave the camp; the MEK refused. After that, they started a psychological war — three hundred loudspeakers. It would drive you crazy, for two years. They blared obscene propaganda, to provoke people to react.

"4/11. U.S. forces were ordered to leave the camp, thirty-six were killed. The U.S. cabled before entry not to malign the police, there would be no violence. The started killing; the shots were with American equipment. The UN never confronted, issued statements of condemnation.

"The UN requested relocation from Ashraf to Camp Liberty; Iran wanted the MEK to leave. Martin Kobler was the UNAME representative. He was German and sinister. As they moved in, they removed the protective T-walls, which protected against explosions. A few months later, the first missile attack occurred. They removed the T-walls to leave us without protection. The last group from Ashraf arrived at Camp Liberty in 2012. The MEK, left one hundred at Ashraf to protect the camp. On 2/13 was the first attack; we had five missile attacks. Each time strengthened us for the next attack. The MEK launched a major international campaign to set up t-walls to the protect camp. There were many congressional hearings; 141 residents were killed during attacks, twenty-seven died during the medical siege.

"After the attack on Ashraf, Brett McGurk, wanted to become US ambassador to Iraq. As a special representative of the president, he came to Camp Liberty. We showed how no one could get into Ashraf without Iraqi knowledge. McGurk said Iranians were not in cooperation with Iraqi forces."

The Youth

Speaker #1

"I am twenty-nine. I found out about the MEK when I was eleven years old. During my last year in high school, I received my biology diploma, and was accepted to university in the graphics field, art, biology. My parents were political prisoners. My uncle was executed. There is a dictatorship in Iran. I saw scars of torture on my parents' bodies. I've seen public executions, child labor, begging, selling kidneys to rent a house. Human beings have a responsibility to be free. if you don't have a choice, you are not human. I've known about the PMOI since childhood. Two things helped make my decision. 1.One, [the] pain my people are experiencing. Two, I became familiar with the PMOI. I was watching satellite TV, seeing different people who are educated, some abroad, that left that life to fight for PMOI. They are fighting for us. How can you sit here while others are fighting for our freedom? "The savior is in the mirror", someone who wants to change the situation. At Ashraf, my sister who is older joined the PMOI also.

"My father came to visit after one year. They arrested him and tortured him for ten years. His cancer treatment was prevented. They kept him there until he was to die. After an international campaign, he was released after the eleventh year. I saw the Ashraf attacks — the 2011 rocket attack. I lost friends. My aunt was shot in the heart. This is the price of freedom. Freedom is not free. Our love to our people is the idea that gives us the strength to continue our way. We are close now…I am proud of her position. We are the only answer to the Iranian regime — democracy, moral values is the answer to the Iranian regime. Dictatorship can be answered. We try to contact young people in Iran. We work on our own computers, especially after the last uprising. People want to know about the PMOI. We use Telegram, Twitter, Instagram, to ask about the future program for Iran. We go after twenty to thirty years old, women."

Speaker #2:

"I am thirty-six. At six months old, they executed my father, aunt, two uncles. I was in prison for two years at Evin. It was a very hard situation, hard on a baby's mother, so my grandmother raised me. I grew up with her for five years, then my mother came back from prison. It was not a normal life. It is hard to think about. I decided to have normal life; I had everything. One of my best students, in mathematics, wanted to be a doctor. We couldn't close our eyes to the situation in Iran. I opened her eyes and we chose the PMOI. This the reality when you speak to any member of the MEK. I consider it my greatest honor to have the fortune to join the MEK. Speaking as a young woman, I could have had a great personal life. But, I think I am the most successful as I am not after personal success but success of other Iranians. You many know that during my years at Ashraf there were many ebbs and flows, many challenges. Perhaps you may want to ask…what inspires us…to stay in MEK, given the risks. It's not an easy life.

"What initially prompted me to join the MEK as a girl? I was full of vengeance. I wanted to have an opportunity to fight against the regime, avenge their loss. But when I joined, I must tell you that this path was so difficult, the regime was so brutal, that at some point I felt the motivation for revenge was not strong enough to carry forward our struggle. I can tell you from personal experience what enabled us to persist and move forward with my fellow sisters and brother was love, because revenge is not strong enough to keep you going. The key was love for each other and for fellow compatriots in Iran. I want to share with you a memory of an incident in 2009, during the uprisings. One of my responsibilities from Ashraf was to receive video from Iran and disseminate on social media…of course, clips. I would receive and watch them; they were very shocking and moving. Troops opening fire, beatings, when I was watching those video clips I repeatedly told myself it wish it was me that was targeted and why aren't we in Iran and why can't the MEK act as a shield. Interestingly enough, a few days later at a meeting in Ashraf we were discussing videos, one of our brothers got up and went behind the microphone, saying — when I saw video clips I had a sense why wasn't I there to defend them?

"I said to myself how strange this person had exactly the same feelings from inside Iran. This is that ideal, that value, that element, that has inspired us to join the MEK, to join the MEK and motivate us to stay and persist in spite of all the difficulties we have experienced all these years. That value is love and selflessness for others without any expectation of return for what we have done. When asked about negative propaganda, you know we are the third or fourth generation. During the time we spent in Ashraf, we have been interviewed many times by Iraqis, UN,

Americans. We were told in privacy, we were told, leave Ashraf and we will get you outside of Iraq. We always said one thing — that is, we told them we have consciously chosen to give everything we have so that Iranians are free. In a sense for us, the opportunity to be in the MEK is something we have gained, not something we have lost.

"We are not lamenting we are deprived of some things. We are the receivers. Do you really think it is possible to keep us, the younger generation under the direct fire of bullets, missiles, clubs, et cetera? That is not possible…we are not ignorant, we are all educated Iranians, computer programmers, university students, as were others. We have good social status. The question is — perhaps you can keep someone against their will for two decades? Do you think it is really possible to keep someone here?

"Do they look forward to a new life? For now, we are singularly focused on bringing down this regime. We have devoted our entire energy to overthrowing this regime, not to just think about at this point. I will share with you some of the dreams…I have seen a lot of photos from Iran, a lot of children wandering around Iran. No one to care for them. It is emotional. A lot of women, girls, to survive, prostitute themselves, sell body parts to survive. The thing that has always been a source of joy and happiness is that we and others can return to Iran, and take care of these children, bring to reality the dreams that they have. Have you ever had the feeling of helping another person, when you see them happy, how fulfilling and happy you are? I think this is the greatest moment of happiness for any human being and I can tell you I am biding the time to come to that point. I have the image of one of these little kids on my desk, I always look at him, and tell him wait, we are going to get to you soon. Of course, there are thousands of those kids.

"We have a lot of work to do, therefore I feel very happy here, because I know what I want to achieve and we will be even happier. I am a video producer, computer programmer, work on social media. Indeed, we do communicate with others in the West, people who know about hacking, filtering, for us to get their support and help. We have to tell them what we are doing and why we need their help. In fact, many come and contact us and ask us about some of the posts…images, etc.. They question us what is this about, what does this say, and we explain to them. They say we support what you are doing, also given that news coming out of Iran is censored, the MSM doesn't report much. We disseminate what we receive from our contacts in Iran. I haven't had any shadow banning on Twitter. It might be in cases of others. To give an idea, in 2009, we would of course put a logo of our website on a clip and gave to MSM. CNN broadcast with the logo on it. In 2018, during the uprising, Reuters got a lot of video from us."

Speaker #3:

"I joined PMOI in 2000. In Iran I didn't know anything, and was prohibited to talk about the MEK, even mentioning PMOI was a crime. This was the regime's red line. I didn't know anything. I got to know by my father, a political prisoner, because he was an MEK supporter. Khomeini started to suppress freedom from the very first day in all aspects of society. He executed

120,000 MEK; he found the MEK the main obstacle. Those executed accepted the most barbaric brutal torture and crime; they refused to kneel and surrender. I had no idea, my father was the one. I became much more curious, watched the satellite channel, began reading the website. Although the regime made it very hard to reach, censorship, noise, filtering jamming, they moved and repressed stories of the MEK. As a teenager at thirteen, I had many dreams. I had a wealthy life. My father was a surgeon, and the owner of a prosperous construction company, with an annual income of several million dollars. I loved completing my education. Seven of my aunts and uncles live in the U.S.; many of my cousins graduated universities, had an opportunity to live in the U.S. in the best conditions. When I saw what was in our society I felt guilty; felt pressure. There are no minimum standards for people to live with dignity; my people are not free to choose their clothes. The hijab is compulsory, selling organs, etc. I saw all this but didn't know the rich history against this. I didn't know the solution. Eventually I found the solution in the MEK. I was most dedicated to the cause of the Iranian people's freedom.

"They left everything they had in their lives to make their people free; they made the decision to join the PMOI. I joined along with family, the greatest honor in our life. We have achieved our dignity as human beings, facing the dangers, risks. Human being means being responsible towards others. Human being means sacrificing for other people. We find all these values in the MEK, the greatest honor in our life. What I used to hear of the MEK, the reality is much more, a chance for real freedom and a prosperous future for Iran with the MEK. The values that the Iranian people really need — gender equality young and old, poor and rich. It moved me, made me join the PMOI. Thousands of people have left all dependencies and interests in order to fight with everything to fight with the MEK to make them free. This was moving for me, I've been here for nineteen years, there hasn't been two equal days that have been the same. Every day is different from the previous one; every day I learn something new. When you listen to stories you are moved and impressed from humility and humbleness after forty or fifty years, they are not done yet; this is truly moving for me. I was fourteen when I joined, and I work in social media."

Speaker #1:

"I was chatting with a worker who had been toiling for thirty years, who had [a] bad life, no salary, hours and hours in a line for food, after one hour crying about pain, he is sure we will never give up.

Speaker #4:

"I joined the MEK in Iran. I am thirty-one. When I joined I was eighteen, an agricultural engineering in Iran. I was also accepted in nuclear physics, but I chose agriculture. Of course I always thought about how I can get to Camp Ashraf. I have a large family all of whom sympathize with the MEK. A hundred member Nabivi family in different cities. Many members of the family are right here in Ashraf 3. There are thousands of others like my family who really have affection and love for the MEK, many members were executed. All are very well-educated, my uncle provided help to many.

"My neighborhood was an MEK district. In this city, the regime changed the name. All of them who were killed in Iran, they know their support for the MEK was consciously chosen, they knew the price, the paid the price. Another uncle, I loved him very much. There was a strong bond between uncle and nephew. I was seven years old when the MOIS attacked our home. I knew nothing about the MEK, they came and searched the entire house, arrested my mother, father, uncle, took my sister toddler, took her with him. She is in Iran. She has a master's degree in industries; they took everyone. I had no clue as to why they were doing this. It was very scary.

"That incident prompted me to think as to why is this happening here. My father was imprisoned for two years, exiled to a remote city in Iran. Both of them were exiled to the city of Yas in central Iran. These were difficult years for us as father was not with us. My uncle also. Of course, in order to see him, we traveled a long way to see him in Yas; it took us seven hours. When he returned from years of exile, he had to sign up with the authorities whenever he wanted to go. I kept asking myself why did my father and my uncle sign up? What kind of problems did they pose to the regime for this? Why is that significant?

"My father's cousin has spent thirteen years in prison; he is now here. He's been here thirteen years, a survivor of the 1988 massacre. Another one is in prison for fourteen years, another six years in prison.

"It's interesting whenever there was some sort of rebellion, unrest, security agents would attack our house and take computers. Once on anniversary of the rebellion, during a presidential election, and on other occasions as well. So I saw all of these constant attacks for the simple reason my father and others supported the MEK. There are only three thousand MEK, why do they pose such a huge threat to the regime, with massive military and security forces? As I grew up, I visited websites, history, activities, et cetera. I also read about stories of the 1988 massacre. In 2005, my grandmother and grandfather, two uncles, my aunt, three uncles, aunt, cousin, father, came to Camp Ashraf to see another aunt. When they came, they were heavily impacted by what they saw. When they came, they were happy to see my aunt, but what was more interesting was a set of relationships at Ashraf and the kindness they received. I wanted to come but I didn't come, but the MOIS again attacked our house. They went to each and every one of their houses, even grandmother and grandfather who are elderly, they interrogated for twelve hours. The MOIS, realizing how interested the family was in the MEK, and concerned the younger generation would join the MEK in Ashraf, at sixteen, the MOIS summoned me for questioning.

"My family was continuing at Ashraf. The interrogator said, the Americans/UN are telling you, your future is ahead of you, why don't you leave, why don't you go to university? Me and my cousin Mariam, we asked him are you serious about this? University has quotas, and our family has a relationship with the MEK.

You would allow us to enroll? He tried to shed crocodile tears for our future.

"Let me ask you, with everything that I told you, do you still intend to go to Ashraf? I looked him in the eye and said yes. He said then I'm going to make life very difficult for your father. Yes, my family is very involved with the MEK but I chose myself to join the MEK. Every term I was getting perfect scores, I loved to study at university. But, I want to tell you what prompted me to realize my first choice has to be the MEK. I was a freshman, I always thought to myself there is something I haven't done. I wasn't satisfied to go to the university. I was studying but I felt that is not my ultimate goal; of course I was studying the MEK's sites. One video I saw, an MEK woman fighter was firing her weapon. Another woman that I saw, a political prisoner, eighty-six, came to the U.S., lost her left leg. She told her story to the media. I said to myself, how powerful are these women. Amazing they had such prominent positions within the MEK.

"Walking in the streets of Qom, the vice squad approached a young girl, why are you wearing this type of a dress? They were trying to force her to tighten up her scarf, present more modestly. When at the university the morality police would watch girls' attire, etc. On one hand, I saw how the mullahs treated Iranian women, and how the MEK treated Iranian woman. But what really was a turning point was a speech I saw on satellite TV. Madam Rajavi on International Woman's Day in Paris, 2004. Rajavi, while she was speaking to large audience, openly talked about the process in the MEK where woman had advanced. She spoke sincerely about problems woman had with relationships in the MEK.

"For me it was eye opening. This organization was not hiding anything form the public. It was a fresh face, young fresh girl, red faced I saw on TV. That is when I decided to come to Ashraf. In winter time I left the university. There was lots of snow. There were telling me no cars to get to Ashraf. But I tell you, I felt proud when I made that choice to come. During some moments I had second thoughts, but I was determined to make this a one-way journey. So when I did arrive, for me the key thing was the set of relationships men and women had in Ashraf, At the border crossing, there was a hill, bushes were on the hill. A group of Kurds was in the area, who wanted to cross. We were all together. The border guards approached us. The Kurds were riding horses. The horses jumped around when the security forces came. As horses came towards us, we had to hide in the bushes. So while we were hiding, the security forces found us.

"They put a gun to my head. 'What are you doing here?' They asked for ID cards. When he saw my ID card, at that time several of my family members were in prison. They sold their homes for bail. 'The name sounds familiar,' he said. My heart was popping; God I hope he doesn't know who I am, I said to myself. No, I have to go to Ashraf. But we came with a smuggler who said, 'These guys just want to go to Iraq to see relatives in Iraq.' Ultimately, we were lucky and they let us go, and I got to Ashraf.

"At every checkpoint, even in Iraq, they would ask us. Americans were at the gate, they would know, how to get in. When we got to the Iraqi side, the Kurd drove us. Then an Iraqi MEK supporter brought us to the Ashraf gate, and friends came and took us in. I came with my cousin Mariam; she and I decided to come by ourselves. No men, to assure we as women can do this. We can stand on our own. It was a source of tremendous pride from Arak in central Iran, to Ashraf, six to seven hundred miles.

"When I came and stayed there for a while, I saw relationships that existed which were honest and sincere. If you will, a pure set of relationships. Why can't we have this among the Iranian people? When we were coming, maybe one-hundred that wanted to come to Ashraf, had emailed. The security services had gotten hold of the email and prevented them from coming to Ashraf. Because the regime was so fearful they would come to Ashraf, the mullahs pressured the Iraqi government to relocate Ashraf to Camp Liberty. You know Iraqi forces took control from the U.S. Army after the 4/11 attack on Ashraf. I don't know if you understand, but when you share the same goal, ideal, you develop very profound love and affection. So we have so much love for each other and are willing to give our lives for each other.

"During the 4/8 attack, I lost one of my best friends, shot by Iraqi forces. We had nothing to defend ourselves, only prepared some handmade shields. When we got out of car as Iraqi forces were attacking us, I lost my shield, she gave her shield to me. I refused but she insisted. She was shot and killed. Iraqis used armor and live fire, killed thirty-six MEK, eight women, men. All the woman who were killed, it was extremely painful for me. Not a day goes by without me thinking about them and remembering their faces. I want to tell you, we haven't come here for our personal goals, we did so for lofty ideals and they gave their lives for these ideals. There are thousands of women who live in extreme poverty, and so given what I know about other women, I don't think about what I gave up. I am not questioning my decision; my singular focus is to do what needs to be done to overthrow the regime and bring freedom back to our country, a nation for where forty years the regime has destroyed everything. Should I not be singularly focus on changing the situation? You asked about life after the overthrow, but before that we have to be focused on the overthrow! We saw the 2018 uprising in Iran; they don't want this regime. At the same time, the regime suppression is very harsh. But I can tell you, the regime is on its last legs, weak and vulnerable. It is us the MEK who will deliver the final blow. Who can deliver this final blow? The MEK, and Iranian officials acknowledge. In a sense, I am the MEK and the MEK is me, for that reason we are determined to achieve our goal and achieve freedom in Iran."

Speaker #5:

"My father was a political prisoner, and myself for one year. I've had an extraordinary life, the best unit in science and technology; I was learning metallurgy, engineering. I had my hopes, normal hopes. During the 1999 uprising, I was a witness. I was a beautiful girl, with a nice life with a father [who was] a dentist. I saw intelligence agencies, saw what they did to university students. Throw them out windows of the dorm, blood on the street. But despite everything that was done, people were propagating that reformers were the path to the future. Two students began a publication; I saw they were arrested. Secret agents at the university identified and arrested them. They were told they should cease publication, and held them for a week in cages, put under psychological torture. If you don't stop, we will kill you. In my mind, no way, expressing an opposing view and not being killed. I was always feeling uncomfortable and agonized, seeing impoverishment, pressures exerted on university students. But, I could not think of any solution to rectify the situation until 1999 when I got to know about the MEK. I think it was that year, I found what I was looking for. For all my university friends, it looked unnatural to join the MEK, because I couldn't even sleep in a dorm with other girls as I had certain principles from our family life. Although when we were young, my father would help the poor, but because he was very wealthy, we had a very comfortable life. I tremendously enjoyed traveling, university, taking advantage of amenities as we had money, but if you are a human being, you cannot have all these good things to yourself, so in the MEK, I saw a group of people who want these good things of life for every Iranian. So for us, given what we know about the MEK, it was very easy to choose to come and join the group.

"One time, some of our aunts told us to go abroad — why don't you come and join us? So we told everyone else we were going to live abroad, as if the regime were to find out it was Ashraf, they would have prevented us. We came to Turkey and got a visa and came to Iraq. Nineteen years have passed, I came in 2000. Of course this was a short period, but a lot happened afterwards. Let me tell you about the sixteen years prior to Albania. Because of restrictions against Ashraf, we embarked upon a program to train residents of Ashraf to become self-sufficient. At Ashraf, we had university. We studied electrical engineering at Ashraf, for two years. We had on the job training, we were responsible for generators, EE issues. At Ashraf, of course because medical treatment was an issue for us, we received training for medical care/assistance. Physicians and nurses were already there, they began to teach. I'm among fifteen who received training to become a dentist, four years of dentistry. I also did dental work under the supervision of my dad, a dentist at Ashraf.

"American officers were surprised at the high morale of all of us. Initially when they set up a TIFF for those who wanted to defect, they thought many would go there, but the exact opposite would happen. They would all tell us about a great world, Europe and America, freedom village, of course they focused on us because we were young and talented. Use your talents in the free world, they said. I think because from their perspective of normal life in West, I sometimes thought to myself, I could understand why Iranians would appreciate. I never thought American officers would think this is the right thing to do.

"If Ashraf stands, the whole world will stand. Of course we had faith as leadership was saying, but we hadn't experienced it. But now after so many years, enduring so many years, when we see that others like Giuliani, Bolton are so supportive, we realize our leadership was right. Senator Torecelli says he would become a member of the MEK. He came to see Ashraf first; he thinks the honor is his. Before they even came, you take Ashraf 3 for granted. You don't realize how important it is. The world changed because of the MEKs perseverance. This is something we never thought would happen — a change in attitude of others outside of our movement. And yes, freedom will come to Iran. Some tyrannies hold their ground but all of a sudden will collapse. The number of people to do this takes one thousand people, but we are three thousand, so because we have that ideal, freedom of Iran will come. We are inspired, we want to take maximum advantage of the time we are spending together. There are a group of us, women and men studying architecture; we have a couple, man and woman who are teaching us. So while we have been waging fight for a free Iran, we have tried to improve our educational skills, as we have many plans for the future of Iran. Normal people think about the next vacation. When they look at us, they think our lives are monotonous, but we are always living with our hopes and plans for the future of Iran. We are thinking about the schools we have to build. For those who have been hit by earthquakes, we have to build homes that will not crumble.

"We enjoy thinking about that future; every human being will live life long or short, but it is not quantity, you have to take maximum advantage of time on this earth, as this is what will remain.

"Freedom for the world's future… this is the message and ideals that count, because we believe in God, we want our lives to be Godlike. So God sent values: freedom, equality, values we cherish and enjoy fighting for and I must tell you the prominent position is not feminist, it is because our believe in equality for a gender that for centuries has been discriminated against. We need women in leadership to free those energies and talents in society, so we are extremely proud to have Madam Rajavi in the National

Council of Resistance in Iran (NCRI), and her belief in equal participation of women in political, social, economic life. I'm sure you
recognize this causes enormous respect to be bestowed upon her.
So I think personally the international community must recognize
the NCRI and Madame Rajavi as president-elect, more than it has
done in the past.

"Because before recent times, appeasement acted as an imped-
iment to our efforts. As you know, we were on the terrorist list,
which was ridiculous. it was the Iranian people who paid the
price. The world has to feel some shame for pursuing this policy.
Now times have changed. The international community must roll
up its sleeves and do what is needed to be done regarding the regime in Iran.

"A Persian proverb, whenever you can cut your losses, you will
get ahead, so each and every one of us, myself included has
stretched our hands to support the U.S. to end the policy of appeasement so we can achieve what people of Iran deserve. When
Iran is free, when we right history, anyone who has done anything
to help freedom will come, the names will be recorded on the right
side of history."

The National Liberation Army

Masoume:

"We were twins...I am Masoume, forty-nine, born in Tehran. I lost my father to illness at five. My mother raised us. My uncle was a political prisoner under the Shah, and we had a natural tendency to be supportive of the MEK. Post revolution in '79, we were active with meetings, gatherings of the MEK. We were young, selling books, leaflets, but after [June of '81], my aunt was arrested, then three uncles, then my mother. At that time we were in high school, the situation was very tough. I remember the night my mother was arrested, the winter of '82, at midnight, the IRGC attacked our home. We went to open the door. Through the glass door we could see them come in with their rifles. They searched the house. Myself and my brother were horrified as to what was going to happen. As if we were hiding a weapon or something, they wanted to destroy the wall with a sledgehammer. My mother insisted we were not hiding anything but they didn't listen. They took my mother, said they couldn't leave us alone and to go to our grandmother's home. They took us to a car, took us to my grandmother's home; my grandmother was horrified. So when she saw us, she realized what was happening.

"I was crying, but grandmother was insisting to the guards why are they taking their mother. My mother expressed support for the MEK they told her and the guards said they would bring her back in the morning. They said the same thing for my uncle. In the morning, there was no word, and then it was clear she had been given a three-year sentence. So it was a hard time as the same night my uncle was arrested. They kept him waiting for Mother in the car. In that year, within a period of five or sixth months, six members of my family were arrested, and another uncle. Not a single night IRGC guards did not come to our home. My brother, grandmother, many children, children from aunt and uncle were arrested. In order to see her, at 4:00 a.m., we had to wake up to go to a new town, Ghezel Hesar prison. They knew us very well, but in order to disturb us, they said we must bring ID proof she is your mother. For example, when we went to meet her in person, the IRCG was right next to us...each time they said come take your mothers stuff away. They would fake and say they killed her, to destroy our morale. Twice they brought a bag of hers, to say she was dead. We would say nothing, they could see how we felt. After three years, our Mother was released. Under all this pressure, we couldn't stand forcing to be religious, I couldn't go to school freely as I was being followed by the mullahs agents. I always wondered if the situation for women would come to an end or not. In '88, despite Mother not wanting me to leave, we did not let her know, friends got me out of Iran. I was forced to cross the border alone. First I say that I did not know what the future would be for me. On the way out of Iran, we were trapped by the IRGC. It was a horrible night for me; they shot at us, myself and another guy. We just split as we couldn't come together because of the darkness. Then I went to local people in that area, they helped me to cross the border, and I crossed into Pakistan. A guy with me was arrested, executed, in the mountains, from Pakistan. I came to Iraq and joined the MEK.

"It was all my wishes to live with MEK, then I joined the National Liberation Army (NLA). I participated in action against Iran, different maneuvers. I took classes for the NLA. Of course, I did not contact my mother. A video tape of a parade was distributed and my brother saw me on video and was encouraged to come and join the MEK. I always wished I could bring my brother in the beginning, but I couldn't do so. When I heard he was here I became very happy. Many of my friends who were with me in Iran were executed. I really wish that I was able to watch all these women and mothers that were in a bad situations and suffering in my homeland; in my mind would have not have been possible to do. When I joined MEK, all the impossible can be made possible and be done. I never, as a woman, thought I could carry a gun and fight for freedom, but when I joined the MEK, it was possible for me. When I came I saw a woman commander with many men under her command. We could drive tanks, do many things. In the first site, only men can do these jobs, but now I see there is nothing that a woman cannot do...anything now we can do — imagination, and we can believe, we can do. This is my deep belief now. Now, if I believe anything is right, I can do it. And, I'm able to transfer such a feeling to all the women and girls in Iran who are under pressure.

"I know women can carry loads to be paid, or small girls forced to get married to elderly men. These reactionary men they do anything to women in the name of Islam. I wish that one day, I will see the smiles of these girls or suffering mothers, even if I think I will be alive at that day, this is my wish and I pay the price, anything. I've had thirty years in the MEK and really enjoyed that. It is the only organization with particularly women who are standing up to the mullahs in Iran. This feeling has been transferred to the Iranian population as the forefront of demonstrations are women. I believe I can do it. My first lesson was the AK-47…how to clean, until the time of shooting I [had] no idea of the kick. I just closed my eyes and pulled the trigger. Then, I realized the kick was nothing. Then, I was on a tank crew, the Chieftan, T-72, Cascavelle, BMP, T-55.

"In [April of '91], the MEK dispersed along the Diyala Province, along the east border. We were not a target, but the Iranian regime assumed this was an opportunity to route us. In late march, a major offensive commenced into the northeast with divisions of the IRGC, dressed in Kurdish clothing. Saying they were Kurds, the IRGC came well into Iraqi positions. The MEK destroyed, captured, and interviewed them. A lot said, why are you wearing Kurdish clothes? They could accuse of MEK of killing the Kurds. It was a defeat so glaring Rasfanjani said he tried to climb a wall taller than our ability. Operation Pearl was part of that operation. This is where the story of killing Kurds started. We invited the ICRC but they refused. Two major differences between the IRCG and the MEK — We were volunteers and committed to our cause. On the other side, the Iranian army had conscripts, from poor villages, uneducated, only in it for the money, or coerced."

Alireaz Rashadi:

"The final MEK foray into Iran. On 7/88, shortly after the cease fire, Operation Eternal Light, penetrated Iranian territory 170 kilometers and captured several towns. The regime brought trucks to the square and told men to get on the trucks, join the fight. To come and join, the regime recruited people by saying if they survived, they would not have to take entrance exam to the university. I studied chemistry, taught calligraphy fine arts, an instructor association said I had nice handwriting; I took part in many exhibitions. Because I grew up in a politically oriented family, I became aware of political environment in Iran.

"I spent a few years with Mother, my mother was always in prison. When my mother was in prison, I would spend a lot of time on Father's side. I never lived together as sister and brother. When mother was released, I spent time with her. She had a lot of friends, all wanted to come to Ashraf. They were all captured and executed in Iran. I could never find a government job, as none of immediately family could have affiliation to MEK, that is why I began to work at a writers association and study at a private university. In 1995, when I saw picture of Mamoume in Ashraf, it inspired me to come to Ashraf. I have been here twenty-two years, a tank driver, BMP, taken lessons for all armored carriers, other armored vehicles. My mother came to see us in Ashraf after the fall of Saddam Hussein. She came three times; she was always jailed two to three months. The last time was for five years. My mother spent her entire life in prison, our family is very unorthodox. In our case, children were far away from the Iranian opposition, yet Mother was spending time in prison. It was not very normal. An interesting point is that the first time she was in prison, she had a child who could visit her. The last time, nobody was left to visit her in prison. But I want to say, first time she was in prison, she was a sympathizer, second, third time she was arrested only because she had come to see her children. This shows how terrified the regime is of a woman visiting her children. They cannot even tolerate supporting an organization she likes, no weapons, ever, never part of any operation. Only because she was a sympathizer, this shows standing of MEK. We are a microcosm of families in Iraq. When they tortured her, flogged her, ripping her, a lash hit her eye, she lost her eyesight; she had no treatment. The MEK issued a statement about my mother.

My uncle was arrested two years later for coming to Ashraf — fifteen years in prison. This was before the 2009 uprising. He was a well-known bizarre merchant, a family from Tabriz, a famous neighborhood Amir Khiz. That's where the leader of the constitutional revolution, khan lived. It is a known bastion of resistance against kings. When they sent Russian forces to suppress Tabriz, except that neighborhood, they defeated the Kayaks, captured Tehran, that's how the constitutional revolution was won.

Ali asked about leaving MEK - my answer is — my stay in Ashraf is twenty-two years, enduring military attacks, American attacks, missile attacks on Camp Liberty. That person cannot be held in the movement against his will. Somebody who takes the risk of crossing the border to join the MEK, as happened to many like us, someone who leaves everything behind, to join the MEK, leaves behind dreams, life, and future, it would be ridiculous to say that he or she being held against her will. I could have been master of writing in Iran, received a high education in Iran. When I hear allegations, we laugh. I was screened sixteen times by U.S. forces at Ashraf, at Liberty, the UNHCR was on top of us every day. Now we are in the heart of Europe, everything is open, what is to keep us here? We have the Internet, can see physicians, my family came to visit five times in Ashraf. We present reality to critics, they have to answer themselves."

Nuclear Weapons

Throughout its history, the MEK has been instrumental in calling out the regime's nefarious activities, whether that be supporting proxy armies throughout the Middle East, bankrolling and executing terror efforts globally, or most importantly, the development of nuclear weapons.

It was the MEK that successfully disclosed secret Iranian nuclear sites in 2020, alerting the world to the advanced nature of the regime's weapons of mass destruction program and agenda.

Successful Completion of the Resettlement of Camp Liberty residents from Iraq to Europe

9th September 2016

Failure of the plan to arrest PMOI officials and to launch missile attacks against Camp Liberty

Simultaneous with growing calls seeking justice for 30,000 massacred political prisoners, the victorious transfer of PMOI members opens a new chapter for the Iranian people and Resistance

NCRI — This afternoon, September 9, 2016, the final group of Camp Liberty residents (more than 280) departed Baghdad, Iraq, for Albania. This final round of departures marks the successful conclusion to the process of relocating members of the People's

Mojahedin Organization of Iran (PMOI/MEK) outside of Iraq despite the Iranian regime's conspiracies, obstruction and threats, which continued until the very last day.

During the four-and-a-half-year-long resettlement process, the residents of Liberty were relocated to European countries, including Germany, Norway, the United Kingdom, The Netherlands, Finland, Denmark, Belgium, Italy and Spain. Close to 2,000 residents left Iraq since the beginning of 2016.

In this process, the religious dictatorship ruling Iran provided red notices to Interpol and used fake arrest warrants issued by the Iraqi Judiciary in a bid to prevent the departure of 1,000 PMOI members, and arrest officials and other well-known figures.

Exploiting the post-invasion atmosphere in Iraq, the ruling clerical regime did its utmost to destroy the PMOI/MEK. Three massacres at Camp Ashraf, five missile attacks on Camp Liberty, two cases of abduction of residents, and the imposition of a full-fledged eight-year siege, which left 177 residents dead, constituted parts of this inhumane, albeit futile, plan.

The goal of the Iranian regime was not to see the departure of PMOI members from Iraq; rather, it sought to annihilate or force them into surrender. The victorious transfer of the PMOI members and regime's major defeat in this regard, which takes place simultaneous with growing calls seeking justice for 30,000 political prisoners massacred in 1988, opens a new chapter for the Iranian people and Resistance.

In its annual declaration, adopted a few days ago, the National Council of Resistance of Iran (NCRI) commended the tireless efforts of its President-elect Mrs. Maryam Rajavi to ensure protection for the safe transfer of Liberty residents outside Iraq. The NCRI said the support extended to the Iranian Resistance by distinguished American, European and Arab personalities provided a political shield for the resettlement of PMOI members, noting that otherwise, the Iranian regime and its Iraqi proxies would not have allowed the safe departure of even a single PMOI member from Iraq.

Over the past year, owing to the efforts of the Iranian Resistance, the United States Congress introduced resolutions and passed legislation, obligating the U.S. Government to undertake the necessary measures to protect the residents of Liberty and to safely transfer them out of Iraq. Similar resolutions and declarations were also adopted in the European Parliament, and in parliaments in the United Kingdom, as well as in other European and Middle Eastern countries.

On July 19, 2016, the United Nations High Commissioner for Refugees stated, "UNHCR is supporting a steady and growing stream of movements out of Iraq in coming months. It is hoped that the process will be completed well before year end. This progress has been achieved with the cooperation of the residents who have proceeded with the relocation process despite difficult circumstances, including the attack on 4 July 2016, which fortunately did not result in any casualties."

The UNHCR added, "Ongoing success in the implementation of solutions has also been assisted by the residents' commitment to meeting the bulk of the associated costs, particularly for long term support of all residents relocated out of Iraq who have no access to state-sponsored assistance."

In the course of the process to resettle Camp Liberty residents, Iraqi intelligence agents, acting at the behest of the Iranian regime's ambassador to Iraq (a commander of the terrorist Quds Force), prevented the residents from taking with them their personal belongings, such as computers, radios, cell phones, and even electric shavers. The agents confiscated 255 personal computers today and yesterday, alone. The residents strongly urge the UNAMI to take back the computers and send them to Albania at the first possible opportunity at the expense of the residents.

On the other hand, despite its previous commitments, the Iraqi side prevented the sale of over 90 percent of the residents' property. The residents had signed a contract with a government-approved Iraqi merchant to sell their property for $10.7 million. But, in the end, Iraqi agents only allowed the sale of 10 percent of the property at one-fourth of the market price.

Previously, during former Iraqi Prime Minister Nuri al-Maliki's tenure, $550 million worth of residents' property at Camp Ashraf was seized and placed at the disposal of the Iraqi military and militias. The Iranian Resistance underscores its legitimate right to legally pursue this matter in courts in order to receive commensurate compensation for the property.

In recent weeks, the clerical regime's Quds Force provided an assortment of missiles to, and tasked three of its Iraqi proxy groups, Kata'eb Hezbollah, Asa'eb Ahl Al-Haq, and Harakat al-Nujaba, to launch missile attacks on Camp Liberty at the earliest possible opportunity. On August 19, 2016, Kata'eb Hezbollah stationed a missile-equipped truck at a location near Camp Liberty. But the plan to attack was discovered and thwarted by Iraq's Federal Police.

Secretariat of the National Council of Resistance of Iran

September 9, 2016

The Regime Weakens but Fights to the Death

Speaker #1:

"The number of demonstrations in 2018 doubled [from] 2017. Khamenei was weak, unable to make decisions on the economy.

"50 million live below poverty line — explains why [there are] body parts for sale. The official government figures, six million unemployed, forty percent university grads, three to seven million [involved in] child labor, two million in the capital, Tehran.

"Government subsidies have continued' the equivalent of 450,000 riyals is $3.50 per month per person. A monthly salary [of] 12mm riyals is 120 dollars per month. Prices of basic goods have risen astronomically. A family of four paid every month, 375 dollars. This is fourteen million Iranian workers, 56 million Iranians live below poverty line. These are regime economists. Production units are being shut down. The workers say we are slaves, hired on temporary contracts, not insured. Eleven million temporary workers, regime controls body parts network. The price is 450 dollars for a kidney, about 180 dollars to person for sale. The regime is making money off people's body parts. In 2018, thirty of the longest running factories were shut down. Iranians know very well that the source of disaster is the mullahs. Out of 82 million Iranians, only fourteen million have full-time jobs. Ten million part time jobs, forty million inactive, four million looking, led to tremendous brain drain. In 2018, university students left Iran. Iran is 31st in the world in the rate of brain drain, and created constant protest since 2018. How disillusioned — regime had to bake cakes to get people to come to the 40th anniversary of the regime. The regime cannot deal with the situation while it faces an organized resistance. The resistance units are active in this environment, demonstrate what Iranian people want.

Speaker #2:

"Mina Vatani was a political prisoner for five years at Evin Prison, with a death sentence. He was transported to a hospital for medical treatment, but escaped. His family was arrested because of the escape, husband and sister executed, 2 brothers imprisoned for [a] number of years.

Resistance units started 4-5 years ago in Iran; they operate underground. In December of 2017 they came to prominence with the uprising. In the last year, they have become more effective and numerous, across all society. Actions are to support the Iranian people but also aim to break repression, tear down wall of fear, give hope to the public, inspire them to be more active. Many were taken action against posters the regime is guarding. The number in units varies from 2-10, and enjoy support among ordinary Iranians who see their actions. People opened doors of homes, security mobilized large forces.

Rebel cities in Iran, Isfahan, ordinary people express opposition to regime, inspired by resistance of camp Ashraf for 14 years, you can build one Aashraf in each city."

Speaker #3:

"I worked in Vancouver in computer sciences; one of our main tasks here [was to] closely monitor the activity of resistance units. Even the regime's officials express fear of these units. The regime knows how these units came into existence, ward 350 Evin, Ashraf 350, they disbanded the ward, distributed to prevent allowing a center of resistance in Evin Prison. The regime made it look as though no one dares challenge the authority of the supreme leader. The activities of resistance units take away this impression, targeting the supreme leader. Yes, you can challenge the supreme leader, enjoy support; this level of activity caused demoralizing activities, defections, caused Iranians to want to join resistance units in Iran. In fact, Khamenei recently said he would manage public information to prevent news of resistance Units actives becoming public. In Some cases of the regime opened fire on units; they shot and killed one unit who wanted to post image of Madame Rajavi. The prisons are now the center of opposition in prisons. They are released if they pay large bail, some cases put on trial, and they admit supporting MEK."

Speaker #1:

"Resistance units are not spontaneous. They are the culmination of a forty-year struggle, and there has never been a breaking point; this entails several generations, many executed. Resistance units continued for three generations in Iran; they are present everywhere you see a protest. The MEK is there...they organize, direct, coordinate protests. The regime calls them organized, understands their voice reflects outside of Iran. The resistance units realize the policy of appeasement has gone wrong; it is a good opportunity to expand in Iran. This is a key point for the international community to stop giving the regime resources, stop appeasement.

"The regime's reaction to rebel units is that nobody is permitted to mention the MEK at all. They only call them hypocrites. The IRGC commanders are now publicly talking about the resistance. In 8/18 they said the MEK is relying on resistance units, beware of the day they get weapons. We have mobilized the youth in Iran. The MEK network in a short time organizes social protests, and the possible capture of weapons depots. The MEK is calling Iranians to the streets. The MEK mentioned Iran state media, parliament as targets.

"420,000 MEK members are taken each year are taken as prisoners. Some are in temporary detention, some receive heavy bail with a trial date. Others are seeing time in prison. In January of last year, 8,000 were arrested. This is the year of shame; the prison population is overcrowded, with no food, medical, sanitary. The regime's henchmen sell narcotics to prisoners, sell drugs to make money. They have no hot water, no warm clothing, many are starving, with 220,000 serving long-term sentences."

Speaker #3:

"The prisoners are used to control society, whenever demonstrations happen, the regime executes them in public. There is a hatred of society towards the regime. There are economic problems affecting prisons; they charge prisoners for maintenance, even heat, families paid for food."

Speaker #4:

"The economy is ruined; due to bankruptcy, wages have not changed. Currency devaluation hurts the poor, the transport fleet is destroyed. Agricultural exports are dying. Water is detoured for the IRGC so agriculture is almost at zero. Food is imported, which the regime makes money on. The regime depleted retirement funds. There is manipulation of the official and black-market currency exchange rate.

"Syria is not going very well, sanctions make it difficult to fund the Syrian war. There is pushback against Iranian involvement in Yemen, Iraq, Lebanon. They bury them in Syria, and have to pay militias.

"Supposed privatizations have devastated the economy. Regime officials are stealing industry. IRGC companies buy a company and sell off the equipment. They purchase with borrowed money from the banking system, with money from the air, a general buys companies.

"The regime is diverting water from the famous Isfahan River. Water now goes to IRGC steel factories. Tens of thousands of farmers are now devastated. Six rounds of protests including front loaders to break the pipes and the regime opened the damn for 20 days. Farmers have turned their back on the clerics — the enemy is here, not America."

Speaker #1:

"We have a massive television effort. Most Iranians watch Visage of a Free Iran. Anyone who is seriously opposed to the regime, watches our program. Before social media, people had to use satellite dishes, which were jammed. People have little opportunity to watch comedy. MEK comedy people watch. Programs are on social media, Telegram, with easy access. Messenger of Happiness is one of most watched programs. Our main news broadcast also. Families invite relatives, lock the doors and watch MEK TV. Social media has made it available. It is a continuation of protests and discontent, and political awareness. When multiplied by organized resistance, it is a tremendously powerful force against the regime.

"We will not be identical to the experience of deposing the Shah. Why? One, we have the experience of the Two, the Mullahs have the IRGC, which is far more savage and barbaric. We need an organized resistance force."

Speaker #2:

"Rebel units include women, young girls, some all-female. There is an enormous attraction to rebel units, with numerous requests to join. News of rebel units has gone to the prisons; when released, the prisoners find units to join."

Speaker #3:

"Each day passing, the regime becomes weaker domestically. MPs are saying they can't even talk to people anymore. Another factor is internal feuding, the regime is paralyzed."

Speaker #1:

"We are focused on expansion units of resistance, protests, and elevating the level of resistance, the agenda of the MEK network inside Iran. We want to link them together, under a unified command. Link them to people who are protesting. The regime is fearing this."

Speaker #4:

"We have not only economic demands, slogans are becoming politicized. They call to release political prisoners, arrest members of the regimes. This impacts ordinary citizens.

"The regime is looking for MEK/US action in 2019. What I can say is that overthrow of the regime is much sooner than much people anticipate. Rebel cities are expanding. This is what of regime is fearful of, expanding to a point where it cannot control.

"The West has to stop appeasing, providing lifeline to the regime."

My Visit To Ashraf 3 — Meet The MEK: Iranian Freedom Fighters Long For Freedom[2]

September 19, 2018

On a recent business trip to Albania, I was invited to visit the new camp of the People's Mojahedin Organization of Iran, or the Mojahedin-e Khalq (MEK), still being built about forty-five minutes outside of Tirana, on the way to the Albanian coast. I accepted the invitation, although I must admit, I had no idea what to expect upon reaching the sprawling facility, which is the new home for approximately 3,200 of the Iranian resistance movement's personnel after being forced out of Iraq by violence from the Iranian-backed government.

I want to write more about the group and its agenda in the near future, but today I just want to explore what I found at Ashraf 3, which is the name the MEK has given the new camp, after the first Ashraf on the Iraqi border, where the group launched raids into Iran almost two decades ago.

With the Trump administration pulling out of the so-called Iran deal, the MEK has been given new hope in its push for regime change in the Islamic Republic of Iran. With the new sanctions biting, in combination with the consequences of the corrupt regime's incompetent management, civil unrest is rampant across

---

[2] Originally posted in *The Washington Times*.

the country. The MEK sees a real chance to force regime change from inside Iran, without needing the use of expensive and already overextended American military force.

With the eventual fall of the mullahs, the MEK wants to finally install a democracy. It was against this backdrop that I visited Ashraf 3 in Albania.

The camp has been quite controversial, primarily due to the regime's view of the MEK as an existential threat. This has caused the mullahs to act out in reckless ways to counter what it sees as its real opposition, even if it is all the way in Albania. This resulted in a foiled bomb attempt at the Free Iran Gathering 2018 in Paris last June, where an Iranian diplomat was arrested, as well as the recent arrest and indictment of two Iranian spies in Washington, D.C. looking to target resistance officials in the United States.

Iranian intelligence agents have been active in Albania, recruiting former MEK members for propaganda purposes and attempting to stain the reputation of the group within the eyes of Albania's people.

The car picked me up at the hotel in Tirana and we made the drive to the camp. The conversation was pleasant enough and we even stopped for some local fruit along the way. But security was very tight; I noticed there were two cars always together whenever we left the camp over the two-day visit.

A local security firm was guarding the location with perimeter defense and car inspections as we entered the gates — where the two MEK lion mascots guard the entrance.

The camp was very large and in various phases of construction. The group had done remarkably well in such a short period of time to recreate what they left in Iraq. There was everything one would expect in a small city — lodging, food service, assembly halls, administrative buildings.

In a short amount of time, I was introduced to the leadership of the group in Albania and we sat around a table in one of the new buildings to get acquainted. What struck me initially was the openness that I encountered. Multiple attempts at journalistic hit pieces had culminated in a recent drone flyover by an adversarial newsgroup from the UK, most likely funded by someone who didn't want the MEK to be successful in its quest.

As the members of the camp knew I had promised to keep an open mind, I was met most graciously. I asked many questions during my two-day visit. All of them were answered in-depth, sometimes with other members being brought in to give a more detailed and complete answer. I was not prevented from seeing or requesting anything. I asked about life at the camp, those who had left the movement, even about the MEK's alleged involvement in the Iranian Hostage Crisis decades before. All questions were met with complete answers.

In fact, I was given a tour of the camp. The facilities were very functional, if not somewhat barren. With the MEK children having been brought out of Iraq to Europe and America in the last decade, the remaining adult members were mostly older, although I did meet scores of a new generation of MEK, male and female, some of whom were in the group of children who were evacuated from Iraq in 2009, only to join the MEK later in life. Many signed up in their relatives' footsteps, to keep their struggle against the regime alive.

On the tour, I was exposed to the robust cooking capabilities that have been built. I toured the medical facility, which had a good amount of equipment and staff trying to do their best with limited resources. Many patients were in various phases of medical treatment as I walked from room to room.

In addition to being exposed to many of the day-to-day locations members would frequent, I also had the chance to talk and interview probably fifty members from all walks of life within the movement. Some of the older, original members were included, as well as the youngest. They all had their own unique story of what led them to join. Many had violence perpetrated on their loved ones by the regime. Many had family members executed. Many had simply given up hope of a decent life in Iran, and now had committed themselves to bringing regime change for future generations.

Many pundits have described the MEK as a cult. I would describe it as a fanatically committed group of individuals who have given their lives for an idea: a free Iran. Each and every one of them spoke about their people, and how they wanted a better life for the Iranian population. This was especially prevalent among the young men and women I met, many who had scars and wounds from the violence at Ashraf, or even within Iran itself. Many had a deep sense of loss and pain from their dealings with the regime — murder, assault, deceit, torture. Their overriding principle was to prevent future generations of Iran from having to go through the same horrific experiences.

The powerful ideal of freedom permeated throughout Ashraf 3. It was the utmost thing on everyone's mind. It is something bigger than themselves. Most of the people I met were highly intellectual and successful in their previous lives. They could have been living anywhere in the West, but they chose, at a personal sacrifice, to join this movement. The younger members knew nothing but the regime and were hellbent on destroying it. I saw a remarkable level of focus and determination. All of the members of the group had a job to do and were singularly focused on its completion.

Each person I spoke with knew exactly what he or she was fighting for and why they had given up so much of their own lives to fight the regime.

Albania has nothing to fear from this group. I did not see any weapons or military training. They want to become good citizens of Albania and to build a life in the former communist country. In fact, it is the MEK who has to be worried about violence. The regime has shown it will stop at nothing to destroy them. Iranian Ministry of Intelligence agents are active in Albania. They are the ones the Albanian public has to fear, not the people in the camp.

There has been much disinformation purposefully spread about the PMOI/MEK. I hope to confront most of it by writing from personal experience from my interactions with the Iranian resistance. This is the first of many reports on the subject.

Epilogue

Today, there exists a massive information operation by the Iranian regime and sympathetic Western press against the MEK. There is also a campaign to kill or capture MEK officials when the opportunity exists. The FBI arrested multiple assassins in New York in recent years targeting NCRI officials.

In 2017, during the Paris annual event of the MEK, law enforcement arrested Iranian terrorists, including an Iranian diplomat, for planning to bomb the gathering, which would have injured or killed hundreds.

In October of 2020, the NCRI revealed secret nuclear sites in Iran where the regime was developing nuclear weapons.

Alireza Jafarzadeh, an NCR representative, said a body called the Organization Defensive Innovation and Research (SPND) had expanded its work since Iran's 2015 nuclear agreement with world powers (known as the JCPOA, Joint Comprehensive Plan of Action) limiting its atomic program, reported NPR.

Jafarzadeh said that the SPND, which he claimed oversees weaponization, was active at a new site in Sorkheh Hesar, east of Tehran, under the supervision of a Revolutionary Guard commander he named as Mohsen Fakhrizadeh. Jafarzadeh displayed aerial images of this alleged new site, and of a second site at Khojir, near Sorkheh Hesar, that he said was producing ballistic missiles.

The images of Sorkheh Hesar showed a compound that has expanded since 2012 and which, according to Jafarzadeh, now houses SPND-affiliated groups, which he alleged had conducted underground nuclear tests, registering the impact of explosions in the same way, he said, as tests conducted in Semnan in 2000. Jafarzadeh said the facility uses ground-penetrating radars and CG-5 gravity meters purchased under another country's name and secretly transported to Iran.

The Albanian government has expelled the Iranian diplomatic delegation due to nefarious activities against the MEK Camp Ashraf 3 in Albania.

The fight for freedom for the Iranian people continues.

Addendum

In September of 2022, a twenty-two-year-old Iranian woman, Mahsa Amini, died in police custody after being arrested by the Iranian regime's morality police. She was arrested for not covering herself per the regime's interpretation of Islamic law.

Officials denied any reports of abuse, but world opinion has come down on the side that Amini was beaten and died from the injuries she received.

The regime has a long history of abusing women — especially young women, who are the bulwark behind the continuing protests against the regime in Iran. Many are killed in prison, executed by guards, and many experience horrendous sexual torture.

In response to Amini's death, Iranian society exploded in protest. As of July 2023, the demonstrations are continuing across Iran, threatening the regime's survival.

According to the MEK, over seven hundred demonstrators have been killed by police, with tens of thousands more arrested.

Yet, the protests continue.

The Iranian people believe they have no future under this regime and have nothing to lose; their bravery in the face of such evil is breathtaking and should be an example to mankind as the world faces the encroachment of tyranny from globalist forces in coordination around the planet.

The pressure was intense on the regime in Iran, and the mullahs enlisted their global appeasers in the West in an attempt to once again destroy the MEK, the resistance the regime fears.

In an unprecedented move, the Soros-connected government of Edi Rama in Albania led a raid on the Ashraf 3 refugee camp compound where survivors of the MEK have been located since they fled the terror in Iraq, where the Obama administration allowed hundreds of MEK members to be executed by Iranian-backed forces in the Iraqi security establishment.

The raid was a surprise development and involved 1,100 Albanian police. The security forces destroyed and stole computers, bashed other equipment, and abused the MEK resident population at the camp.

Pepper spray and tear gas was sprayed directly in the faces of MEK members at point-blank range. One MEK member, a sixty-year-old man, was killed in the attack. Hundreds of others were injured. We have viewed the video of the raid, and the behavior of the police was horrendous and unjustified.

The raid happened after the Biden administration had been reportedly meeting on American soil with Iranian officials in an attempt to restart the failed JCPOA, or Iran nuclear agreement, negotiated by the Obama administration. The agreement did nothing to stop Iran from acquiring nuclear weapons — in fact, it allowed them to eventually do so.

It is reported the raid on the MEK compound was a gift to the mullahs during the negotiations with American officials. Albania is essentially controlled by the U.S. State Department. Nothing happens without their permission inside the Rama regime. Former American Ambassador to Albania Yuri Kim was infamous for interfering in internal Albanian affairs to push the Soros agenda, going so far as to sanction former Prime Minister Sali Berisha without substantiation for attacking Soros and Rama politically.

It was with this backdrop of global events that the MEK planned its annual Free Iran Summit in Paris in early July of 2023. The event was to include an outdoor rally televised worldwide, along with informative panelists for journalists, politicians, and other government officials.

Anti-resistance forces mobilized into action to stop the event from happening, including the U.S. State Department and French officials.

The local Paris court went as far as to ban the outdoor rally portion of the event. However, this decision was overturned by the French national judiciary the night before the rally was scheduled, so it went ahead as planned. (See statements by the NCRI following this Addendum)

The U.S. State Department issued a travel warning in Paris to avoid the event due to threats of violence, as did security officials in the French capital.

Strangely enough, under this alleged threat status, no French police were seen at the Saturday rally for the MEK, which thousands of demonstrators in support of a free Iran attended for hours in the hot sun.

You can read multiple official press releases by the NCRI below concerning the above recent events in the fight against the murderous Iranian regime.

Text of Speech by Mrs. Maryam Rajavi, President-elect of the National Council of Resistance of Iran (NCRI) Free Iran World Summit

July 1, 2023

Esteemed leaders, distinguished dignitaries who have joined us today at the Free Iran World Summit to demonstrate your solidarity with the Iranian people's struggle for freedom and democracy,

You are messengers of friendship between the peoples of the United States, Canada, Australia, Africa, and elsewhere in Europe and the Middle East.

Thank you for being with us today.

With your permission, I will continue in Farsi.

My dear compatriots,

Men and women have journeyed from various countries, exerting tremendous effort to reach the former home of the Iranian Resistance, where Massoud [Rajavi] arrived amidst the intense heat of the summer in 1981. To the disenchanted people in the towns and villages of Iran who are listening to my voice:

Our country, movement, and Revolution have reached a pivotal moment. A seldom-seen opportunity in the history of nations is before us: we either allow the religious tyranny and the mullahs' rule to persist, or we instigate a revolution, topple the mullahs, and establish a democratic republic with the separation of religion and state, thus liberating our people and our nation.

Fate is knocking on our door; what will be our choice?

Indeed, the answer is a revolution, but it carries a hefty price tag. Our resistance has shouldered the most burdensome weight in Iran's history, persevered through the longest of durations, and navigated the most intricate situations. This brings us to the critical question of our time: will the era of devastation and darkness endure? Will the suffocating shroud of the night continue to envelope our homeland?

No, absolutely not! We see with increasing clarity the invigorating dawn of liberation on the horizon. The magnificent destination of freedom is drawing ever closer. Thus, as the heralds of this new dawn, all that remains is one more leap, one more step, one more final effort. Let us rise!

There are those who conjecture that the regime will inevitably retreat following the 2022 uprising. Even as it entangles itself in various harmful activities, it continues to amass wealth for the mullahs. Once again, negotiations, complacency, appeasement, and the mollification of the mullahs may resume, all at the expense of our nation and the resistance.

But here is our response: Go ahead! Experience it for the hundredth, the thousandth time.

The Shah, bolstered by the financial support of the U.S. and Europe, had vast resources at his disposal. He was even awarded the metaphorical badge of the regional policeman. His army fought in Dhofar, and his intelligence services, along with SAVAK, attempted to stage a coup in Iraq. Yet, in the eyes of the Iranian people, his reign had run its course.

Politically and historically, just like the Shah's dictatorship, the religious dictatorship is teetering on the brink of collapse. Just as you couldn't keep the Shah's regime afloat, you cannot prop up the mullahs, not even with crutches, nor by suppressing the Iranian Resistance.

We firmly assert that regardless of whether the JCPOA is active or not, the era of religious fascism has drawn to a close, and the sun of its existence is setting on the horizon of its downfall.

I want to share my remaining thoughts through a verse from the Marseillaise, the French national anthem, drawing inspiration from the French Revolution, as a way to succinctly reflect upon the 42-year Iranian Revolution. One verse from the Marseillaise declares:

Tremble, tyrants, and you, traitors!

The shame of all parties, Tremble!

Your parricidal schemes Will finally receive their prize!

Everyone is a soldier to combat you.

If they fall, our young heroes, The earth will produce new ones,

Ready to fight against you.

To arms, citizens!

Form your battalions!

March on, let's on!

Less than a month ago, Khamenei declared at Khomeini's tomb: "Today, we have thousands of resistance cells in mosques and gatherings across the nation. From these cells of resistance, we witness the emergence of young individuals as defenders of the Shrine [in Syria], as defenders of security, and as Basij militiamen."

Indeed, why would a regime armed with the Revolutionary Guards, the army, the Ministry of Intelligence, the Quds Force, the Basij militia, and various covert agents need resistance cells? Could it be due to the potential for unforeseen uprisings and the progression of a democratic alternative?

Why does he implore governments worldwide to exert pressure on the Iranian Resistance?

Because he senses the impending footsteps of uprisings and the forces of the Democratic Revolution; because the determination of our people to establish a just society surpasses their fear of repression; because each wave of crackdown is followed by new uprisings, each stronger and more dynamic than the last.

Because brave women are leading this uprising, holding high the torch passed down from generations of resistant fighters who endured torture and execution in their struggle against Khomeini's oppressive regime.

This generation of hundreds of thousands of resistance fighters represents an immeasurable force—a splendid generation symbolized by Massoud [Rajavi], whose radiant stars will forever light up the Iranian sky.

Indeed, an organized movement, with its Resistance Units acting as the propelling force behind the uprising, is attracting an ever-increasing number of oppressed individuals with each passing day. This movement has a dual objective: the overthrow of the oppressive regime and the realization of a revolution founded on the principles of freedom, democracy, and equality.

Dear compatriots,

Sisters and brothers,

Did Khamenei and his oppressive forces show any hesitation in their relentless efforts to suppress the uprising? Absolutely not! Nevertheless, they have been unable to extinguish the uprisings that stem from the existing realities on the ground.

Those who lent them support sought to crush the democratic revolution in Iran for their own gains. However, they have ultimately failed. Yes, it is your combined strength that led to their defeat.

Indeed, such power resides in your resounding cry for freedom, causing tremors within the mullahs' rule.

Why do Khamenei and Raisi demonstrate such fear over a gathering taking place 5,000 kilometers away from Tehran? Why do they feel such terror and apprehension?

Some individuals, including members of the French press, argue that this long-distance control exercised by the mullahs is contrary to the principles of freedom of expression and assembly.

As for the advocates of appeasement within the U.S. State Department, who concurrently backed the tragedy in Ashraf-3, it is enough to note that the mullahs waved their turbans and lavished them with commendations.

At this point, I wish to express my profound gratitude to all the groups, parties, and individuals who, despite their varying opinions, have shown solidarity with the Iranian Resistance in recent days. A united front of Iranians, bound by the shared aspiration for a liberated Iran and a truly democratic republic, has the power to weaken religious fascism and hasten its ultimate demise.

But what is the true essence of this conflict? What does it truly represent? It signifies a struggle that lies at the core of the Iranian people's uprising. Once again, we hear the same rallying cries that sparked the French Revolution: liberty, equality (free from hereditary or religious privilege), and fraternity.

Khamenei and his Guard Corps (IRGC) are painfully aware of the forthcoming wave of uprisings. Consequently, they call upon the USA and Europe to intervene, to obstruct the transformation taking place in Iran, to suppress the leaders of the popular uprising, and to limit its basic rights of freedom of expression, assembly, and political engagement under the pretense of security or national sovereignty. Is this truly indicative of the 21st century Europe?

I recall that on March 10, 2011, exactly one month before the April 8, 2011 assault on Ashraf-1, the European Parliament, in a resolution applauding the condemnation of the Iranian regime, stressed that "issues of sovereignty and domestic jurisdiction can no longer be used to shield states from scrutiny over their human rights records."

However, let me share what emerges from the prevailing spirit of the times (zeitgeist):

Appeasement towards the mullahs' regime may lead to more bloodshed among our people and our resistance, it may lengthen the list of executions, and it may fill more prisons. Yet, it will be futile in protecting Khamenei from his inevitable downfall.

Restoring this stagnant regime to its former balance and quelling the ardor of the uprising is an impossible task.

I must reiterate. We neither desire nor have ever asked foreign governments to help our people and our resistance in toppling the regime. Instead, we urge them to cease supporting the mullahs.

We encourage them to recognize how the American people and nations across Europe are expressing their unyielding solidarity with the Iranian uprising.

Pause for a moment to take note of the resolutions passed by the majority of elected representatives of the American people! Observe the declarations made by the majority of elected representatives from the parliaments in 41 countries - totaling 3,600 parliamentarians - who reject both the fascism of the Shah and religious fascism and endorse the Ten-point Plan proposed by this

Resistance. Let us extend our heartfelt salutations to these esteemed parliamentarians!

What crime has this resistance committed? Its greatest offense
is its unwavering commitment to not waste a single day or hour
in its efforts to overthrow this regime. It ceaselessly works towards organizing resistance and fostering uprisings.

The Resistance is formed by steadfast members who have for-
gone the ease of conventional family life, rebelling against a self-
focused, patriarchal culture that promotes an 'I come first' men-
tality. Their lives are pledged to the cause of rebellion and the
quest for freedom.

The Resistance strongly asserts that Iranian women should
have the right to make their own decisions freely, and to equally
contribute to societal leadership.

The group's mantra stands clear: reject obligatory religion,
mandatory veiling, and imposed government.

The Resistance champions the self-determination rights of persecuted ethnic minorities, ranging from Kurdistan to Baluchistan,
and from Turkmen to Arab compatriots. It represents all those
who voice, across the country, "I am ready to lay down my life for
Iran."

The Resistance has taken form to eradicate rampant unemploy-
ment and poverty, afflictions burdening millions of Iranian workers. Indeed, our movement has risen with the intent of ameliorat-
ing the homelessness experienced by one-third of the nation's

populace and the severe plight of the 80% living below the poverty line.

If these endeavors are considered criminal under the suppressive sharia law of the mullahs, under the regime of despotism and dependence, then yes, we confess guilt and accept our actions with honor.

Yet, we will not permit any compromise on the autonomy of the resistance and the sovereignty of Iran for all the wealth in the world. We refuse to abandon our core beliefs, values, battles, and ideals in the pursuit of power.

We shall not endure the slightest hint of tyranny, exploitation, or authoritarian intent, be it from the dictatorships of the Shah or the mullahs. Furthermore, we place no dependence on any foreign power for the liberation of Iran.

Yet, in the midst of Iran's desolation under Khomeini's reign, there are those who kindle the night throughout the year. They traverse from one street to the next, from one city to another, focusing their efforts on centers of oppression, plunder, and demagoguery, and igniting the fires of popular outrage. This nascent hope, this echoing demand for revolution and liberty, has now come to be known as the Resistance Units.

Honorable allies of the Resistance,

As you disperse from here, please relay to every Iranian you meet that you have found the way. Enlighten them that the answer resides in revolution. Assure them that we can - and indeed, must - strive towards this goal.

Frequently, we are asked how we overcome the myriad hurdles and challenges we encounter. Our reply is steadfast: we possess the ability to surmount them all. Mohammad Hanifnejad, the founder of the PMOI (People's Mojahedin Organization of Iran), created this organization from virtually nothing, in defiance of all odds.

In a period when the People's Mojahedin were confronted with tremendous bloodshed, Massoud Rajavi founded the Iranian National Liberation Army. Even amidst the carnage at Ashraf-1, when our movement's core stood on the precipice of obliteration within Camp Liberty's slaughterhouse, Massoud Rajavi established the Resistance Units. The fruits of his labor are manifest in the persistent uprisings we observe today.

Indeed, our movement's history is characterized by groundbreaking initiatives and transformative creations. By acknowledging Massoud Rajavi' steadfast and inventive leadership, we declare that victory and the future are ours.

They question us and our people, pondering how this bloodthirsty leviathan can be overthrown. Our response is clear: through unrelenting resistance, a struggle a hundredfold fiercer, the mobilization of Resistance Units, a revolt, and the Army of Freedom.

Yet, how do we approach this objective?

Through unending dedication and relentless struggle, never pausing, probing every possible path, kindling the fire within each human soul, cultivating emerging resistance, and awakening dormant consciences. We will resist with resolute determination, persevering in the battle until the shackles are broken, until the path unveils itself, and until the walls come tumbling down.

Yes, we can and we must.

Long live the Iranian people!

Long live freedom!

The democratic revolution of the Iranian people will prevail!

The banning of the rally by Iranian expatriates scheduled for July 1, 2023, in Paris amounts to a disgraceful act against democracy, freedom of speech, freedom of assembly, and succumbing to extortion and hostage-taking by the religious dictatorship ruling Iran. This regime, which has continued its rule for nine months solely through a wave of executions, has hanged over 200 victims since the beginning of May.

In a statement to Reuters, the police acknowledged that the rally could "generate disturbances to public order due to the geopolitical context." This is a clear reference to the threats posed by the regime and amounts to kowtowing to such threats.

The clerical regime's pressures on France to impose this ban reveals the mullahs' paranoia over the popular sentiment towards the People's Mojahedin Organization of Iran (PMOI/MEK) and the organization's pivotal role in the nationwide uprising. It also reflects the mullahs' utter fear over the rally organized thousands of kilometers from Iran by the NCRI, which represents the democratic alternative to the ruling theocracy.

The Iran Resistance will employ all legal and political avenues to challenge and file a complaint against this unlawful and unwarranted ban.

Secretariat of the National Council of Resistance of Iran (NCRI)

June 19, 2023

■■

The Victory of Justice to the Benefit of Resistance

Iranians will hold a demonstration on Saturday, July 1, in Vauban Square in Paris.

On Friday, June 30, the Paris court overturned an order banning the July 1 demonstration by the Paris Prefectural Office. It declared the rally in Vauban Square in Paris free on Saturday afternoon. The Court sentenced the Prefecture of Paris to pay the organizing committee of the demonstration a fine of 1500 euros.

By this order, the Court did not allow democracy and freedom of expression to be sacrificed in a deal with the religious fascism ruling Iran. This is a heavy blow to the clerical regime and the policy of appeasement.

Security being a ridiculous excuse, the reality was surrendering to blackmail by a regime that is the record-holder in executions and the godfather of international terrorism.

The experience of the past four decades has shown that appeasement toward this regime encourages repression, execution, and terror. Annoyed by popular support for the PMOI and their crucial role in the uprising and the growing international support for the Resistance, the mullahs ruling Iran tried to involve foreign powers in suppressing the Resistance. They received a worthy response from the Paris court.

The government's arguments for banning the demonstration assumed the Iranian regime might attack it. It is shameful that the right to freedom of speech and assembly be ignored instead of protecting the rally and confronting this threat.

The unjustified and illegal prohibition of the demonstration wasted a lot of sensitive time for the organizers and created many problems in the planning for receiving the large crowd who wanted to participate in the rally. This left a lot of material and moral damage. But despite all the disruptions, the big demonstration of Iranians will be held on Saturday afternoon.

Secretariat of the National Council of Resistance of Iran

June 30, 2023

III

The Sudden Onslaught by More Than 1,000 Albanian Policemen on Ashraf 3, the Martyrdom of One MEK Member

More than 100 people injured due to firing of pepper spray, some of them in critical condition

At the behest of the religious fascism ruling Iran, this morning around 1,000 Albanian policemen attacked Ashraf in a criminal and suppressive onslaught. They broke many doors, closets, and equipment and attacked the residents with tear gas and pepper spray. Many computers were broken or taken away.

As a result of this criminal attack, a member of the Mujahedin-e Khalq (PMOI/MEK), Mr. Ali Mostashari, was killed and more than 100 people were injured due to police firing pepper spray. Many of them are in critical condition and some were transferred to Mother Teresa Hospital in Tirana.

The actions of the Albanian police are reminiscent of the criminal attacks by Nouri al-Maliki forces on Camp Ashraf in Iraq between 2009 and 2015.

The Iranian Resistance demands that the U.S. Government and the United Nations, which have repeatedly guaranteed the safety and well-being of the residents of Ashraf, to condemn this criminal and barbaric behavior and provide the necessary guarantees to prevent these types of outlaw behavior that flagrantly violate many international treaties, including of the Convention Relating to the Status of Refugees, Universal Declaration of Human Rights, and the European Convention on Human Rights. The European Union, for whose membership Albania has applied, must condemn this barbaric attack and hold the Albanian Government accountable for this behavior.

Secretariat of the National Council of Resistance of Iran (NCRI)

June 20, 2023

IV

Head of Government Information Council in Iran announced regarding the 213 Computers Seized in the Attack on Ashraf 3 on June 20:

"Part of the hard drives and casings have been received."

The United States and Albania should clarify whether the MEK's computers have been handed over to the Iranian regime.

Warning against any collaboration with the religious fascist executioners that would lead to the arrest, torture, and execution of the families, prisoners, and supporters of the MEK and the Iranian Resistance throughout the country.

Fars News Agency, affiliated with the IRGC, announced on July 3: "Sepehr Khalaji, head of the Government Information Council, stated on his social media page regarding the return of Monafeqin's computers to the country: 'Part of the hard drives and casings have been received.' Khalaji added: 'They are busy retrieving information, identifying operatives, and the destructive cores and blind spots.' Khalaji also wrote about the results obtained regarding the recovery of computer data: 'The results so far are promising.'"

In the past 10 days, the media and officials of the mullahs' regime have continuously reported on the contacts between the "security apparatuses (of the regime) of Iran and countries such as Albania." This requires a clear position from this government, and we hope that the American and Albanian authorities firmly deny and provide complete transparency and details.

If the shocking news of collaboration with the religious fascism ruling Iran against the MEK, and the transfer of a portion of the 213 seized computers and hard disks in the attack on June 20, 2023, which left one martyr and hundreds of wounded and maimed MEK members, is true, it is a humanitarian catastrophe and a horrific violation of human rights in collaboration with the ruling religious fascism in Iran, leading to the arrest, torture, and execution of families, political prisoners, and supporters of the MEK and the Iranian Resistance throughout the country, as well as to the regime's terrorist activities outside Iran. Undoubtedly, the responsibility lies squarely with the governments of the United States and Albania. Sharing any information about the MEK with the criminal regime in Iran, which has been condemned 69 times for human rights violations by the United Nations General Assembly and other international bodies, is an absolute red line and completely unacceptable, worthy of prosecution in international courts.

Yesterday (July 2), the government-affiliated Mehr News Agency, quoting official statement of the Ministry of Intelligence (MOIS), praised the Albanian police's actions against the MEK and made a series of false accusations against the MEK regarding "intelligence-security contacts with European intelligence services" regarding the MEK's activities in "various Western countries," especially Albania. It also promised terrorism on the Europe's soil, stating that "Iran is seriously pursuing terrorists outside its borders."

Furthermore, according to Hamshahri Online newspaper on June 27t, Brigadier General Esmaeil Kowsari, a member of the regime's parliamentary Security and Foreign Policy Commission, said: "For several months, there have been communications between the security apparatuses of Iran and countries such as Albania, and it has had very positive results."

Secretariate of the National Council of Resistance of Iran (NCRI)

July 3, 2023

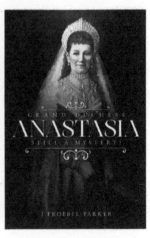